William Porter

Nicotine Explained

Table of Contents

1. Introduction

One of the things that used to frustrate me the most as a regular consumer of nicotine was why I found something that was so bad for me so enjoyable. Humans, like all living creatures, have an innate survival instinct. Animals seem to eat and drink what is good for them, shy away from things that are bad for them, and generally seem to enjoy their lives. Humans however seem to really enjoy and need things that are actively bad for them. There seemed to me to be a fundamental error in me. You wouldn't find an animal in the wild that derived huge amounts of pleasure from eating arsenic (of course such a species would very quickly die out) but it appeared to me that this was analogous to consuming nicotine. Why on earth should we be pre-programmed to enjoy something so much that is so inherently bad for us?

In fact there are good reasons why we end up enjoying nicotine so much, and when we start to dissect and understand those reasons, we can also understand how best to go about stopping. It's rather like trying to work with a computer that you don't really understand. Odd things seem to happen, you try to do one thing and the effect is the exact opposite to what you intended, or something completely unrelated seems to happen. However when you understand it fully, it all starts to make sense and you can start to make it do what you want it to. The human brain is very similar to this, it works in certain ways and when you understand those ways you start to gain far greater control over it. This is particularly true in terms of nicotine, and addiction more generally.

My interest in the mechanics of addiction were first awakened back in the 1990's when, as a teenager, I first read 'Allen Carr's Easyway to Stop Smoking'. For those not familiar with Allen Carr and his series of Easyway books, he developed a very successful method for quitting smoking and then applied his method to various other addictions. Allen Carr influenced me hugely but some of his ideas and theories were, for me, too simplistic, and I personally felt the need for a far deeper analysis to cover the subjects properly. For example, his theory that nicotine does nothing for you other than to cause a 'withdrawal' when it leaves your body simply didn't ring true for me. Nicotine is a stimulant and did seem to leave me feeling more alert. It is my belief that the best way to beat a drug, any drug, is to have as full an understanding of it, and its effects, as possible, be these good or bad. Whilst I believe that Allen Carr was a hugely important pioneer in the world of addiction, I do believe that his ideas can be developed, refined and, most importantly, more fully explained. In 1997 Allen Carr was invited to speak at the 10th World Conference on Tobacco and Health. Unfortunately it did not go well. In his own words he "…could not provide the sort of details and data required by my august audience." I see our understanding of addiction as less of a single answer solution, and more like a baton race. We grab the baton and run with in the limited time we have before passing it on to the next person to take on.

Having said this, you do not need to have read Allan Carr's books before reading this one. The purpose of this book is to be self-sufficient and all encompassing, it doesn't require any previous knowledge or background reading. It uses some of Allen Carr's ideas but develops them and presents them in a different way, it explains how and why they work the way they do, and it introduces some new concepts and insights which, I hope, develop and further our understanding of this topic.

It is worth also mentioning in the introduction that Nicotine Explained is a book about nicotine and nicotine addiction. It covers smoking, vaping, dipping tobacco (snus), chewing, sniffing, patches, pouches and gum. The principles covered apply equally to all methods of consuming nicotine. I have in my time smoked (cigarettes, cigars and even a pipe), vaped, used dipping tobacco (snus), patches pouches (that you put inside your mouth) and snuff so am well versed with all forms of nicotine consumption.

This book is about explaining why people consume nicotine, why they find it enjoyable, and why they find it hard to stop. This is its primary purpose. Achieving this gives us the secondary result; how best to quit. Fully understanding something is the only true way to regain power over it. So by its very nature this book provides a way to quit all forms of nicotine addiction. If this is your primary purpose for reading this book then please note that you have no need to quit nicotine before reading it. This book will dissect and explain the effects nicotine has on us, both good and bad, and it can be very effective to check out everything I say with reference to your own nicotine consumption. Having said this it is not essential to consume nicotine while reading this book, so if you have already successfully quit nicotine then you have no need to start consuming it again.

One of the main positive bits of feedback I get on books is my ability to explain simply and concisely some rather complicated and difficult subjects. I do this by breaking down the entire experience of nicotine consumption into its constituent parts so each chapter deals with a different aspect of it. The problem is that when we experience it, we experience it all together. So sometimes I may go over points more than once, as I explain how they tie in with other elements. When I do this I do try to explain them in different ways as this can give a fuller understanding to a larger number of readers. I have however tried to keep the book as short and concise as possible. I love reading and I think of reading a book as journey. With a work of fiction the journey is the point of the book; it is like going on a cruise where the method of travel is the holiday itself. In that situation you want it to last as long as possible (as I always do when I'm reading a really good work of fiction), but a self-help book is read to obtain knowledge or make a change for the better. In this situation it is the end result that is key. The journey is merely the method by which you get there. So if a good work of fiction is like a cruise, a self-help book is like the cramped economy flight to get to get to the wonderful holiday destination that you have been wanting to get to for so long.

With this in mind let's now cut the preamble and get straight on with the topics in hand. The first of these, unsurprisingly, is nicotine.

2. Nicotine

Nicotine is a stimulant. This means it increases alertness, makes us feel more awake, and increases both heart rate and blood pressure. If you smoke a cigarette, you will be more mentally alert than you were before you smoked it. The problem is however that as nicotine also increases your heart rate and blood pressure, it also has the result of leaving you feeling physically drained, even though you feel more mentally alert. So it has the odd effect of making you feel mentally alert but physically heavy and lethargic. There are several reasons for this, but to fully understand this we need to firstly understand a little about both heart rate and blood pressure.

Heart Rate

Heart rate is measured in BPM, which is 'beats per minute'. This is exactly what is says; it is the number of times your heart beats in a minute. The purpose of the heart, and the reason it beats, is to pump blood around your body. The blood contains red blood cells that carry oxygen and other nutrients around your body, supplying your muscles and organs with the oxygen and nutrients that they need to operate. If you are moving around your muscles require more oxygen, so your heart has to beat faster to meet the demand for extra oxygen.

If you are regularly increasing your heart rate through exercise then your blood composition actually starts to change. Firstly the red blood cells are replaced more quickly, meaning the average age of the cells is younger. The reason for this is that younger red blood cells carry more oxygen and nutrients. Secondly there is a greater concentration of red blood cells in the blood, so every beat of the heart means more red blood cells are reaching the muscles and other organs. This is the main physical difference between someone who is 'fit' and someone who is 'unfit'; it is the different composition of their blood. If your blood contains younger cells that can carry more oxygen and nutrients, and if each pump of your heart means many more blood cells reach your muscles and organs, your heart doesn't need to beat so fast to keep your body supplied with what it needs. It also means you can exercise at higher and higher levels as your heart can easily keep up with the increased activity. This is why doctors are so interested in 'resting heart rates'; they are a clear indicator of the state of your health. The fitter you are, the lower your resting heart rate is.

Now the heart can only beat so fast and as it speeds up, physical activity becomes increasingly uncomfortable and unpleasant. This is your body telling you that your heart is struggling to keep up and that you need to slow down and rest. It is a failsafe mechanism to stop you charging around until you have a heart attack. Obviously exercise is good for you, so this mechanism only kicks in when your heart rate gets to quite a high level.

The problem is that nicotine significantly increases your heart rate and thus the mechanism telling you that you need to sit down and rest kicks in. This is one of the reasons that nicotine consumers tend to be unfit, and why heart disease is so predominantly linked to nicotine. It drastically decreases your desire and indeed ability to do physical exercise, and if you do exercise you will be incapable of pushing yourself as hard . This is also why we like to sit down when we consume nicotine. Yes, we may take nicotine while walking along on occasion, but our idyllic situations usually involve sitting down. If you are in any doubt about this, test it out when you next have your first dose of nicotine of the day. You will feel slightly groggy and out of sorts because you won't have had your nicotine fix, but try to put that out of your mind for the minute. Try to see how you feel physically. How much do you want to sit down and rest, and to what extent are you happy to stand or walk? Are you breathing heavily or normally? What it really amounts to is how strong are you feeling? If a wolf came charging towards you how far could you run before you collapsed? Take the nicotine and compare how you then feel physically while you're consuming it and directly after. See if it doesn't make you feel heavy in your limbs, and far more inclined to want to sit down and rest. Don't take my word for it, try it for yourself and draw your own conclusions. This is caused by the nicotine increasing your heart rate and blood pressure which causes you to want to sit down and rest.

The other aspect of this is that just as regularly increasing your heart rate through exercise makes you fit by causing the age of red blood cells to decrease and for those cells to be more concentrated, regularly increasing your heart rate without exercising does the exact opposite.

Imagine that you are sitting down and your heart is beating at 50 beats per minute, and all your organs and muscles are getting exactly what they need from the blood supply. If you then take a drug which increases your heart rate without exercising, the muscles and organs are then over supplied with oxygen and blood cells. In this situation your body and brain will react and adapt, and it will do this by keeping the red blood cells in circulation for longer (thus the average age of the blood cells will increase) and by reducing the concentration of red blood cells. The overall effect is that your blood will progressively contain lower concentrations of oxygen and nutrients. This process is the exact opposite of getting fit. It is actively becoming unfit.

Blood Pressure

So what is blood pressure? It is literally what it says, it is the force with which your blood is being pumped around your body. It is given as two figures; the first figure (known as systolic) is when your heart is actually pumping, the other figure (diastolic) is the pressure for that short period when your heart rests between beats. Systolic means the phase of heartbeat when the heart muscles contracts and pumps the blood. Unsurprisingly diastolic means the phase when the heart is resting.

Just to give an indication of what is normal, in the UK the NHS states that ideal blood pressure is considered to be between 60-90 when your heart is at rest, and 80-120 when beating (it is measured in 'mmgh' which is a measure of pressure).

The human cardiovascular system works by your heart (which is a muscle) contracting, which forces the blood out of it. There is then a valve which swings shut so the blood cannot flow back into it. The arteries are slightly elasticated so that the heart pumps, the valve closes, the arteries give slightly when the blood flows into them, and as the arteries then squeeze back to their normal size this further assists the flow of the blood.

So what happens if blood pressure is either too high or too low? The arteries through which your blood is pumped are strong, flexible and elastic. They give slightly when the heart pumps, and they have evolved over millions of years to deal with a certain amount of pressure, but if the pressure is too much for too long, several unpleasant things can happen. They can eventually weaken (think about stretching an elastic band to its limit over and over again; it will weaken and eventually snap). The wall of the artery at the weakest point can bulge and eventually burst causing internal bleeding (this is known as an aneurysm).

The other thing that can happen is that the arteries actually start to react to the increase in pressure by hardening. A common theme to this book is how the human body adapts, and if the blood pressure is too high for the arteries then over time the arteries will harden up in order to prevent the arteries from being damaged. This may seem like a good thing, but in fact it isn't for two very good reasons.

Firstly it puts additional pressure on your heart. Think about blowing up a balloon. If the balloon is nice and elasticated then it's easy to blow up, but if you are unlucky enough to pick up one of those balloons that seem to be 3 times as thick as the normal ones, they are incredibly difficult to blow up. Slightly elasticated arteries actually assist with your circulation of blood. As mentioned earlier the flow of blood isn't just about your heart beating, the system works by the heart beating, the arteries expanding slightly, the valve swinging shut so the blood cannot flow back into your heart, then the arteries naturally contracting back to their normal size which provides additional force to move the blood. If the arteries start to harden they aren't giving the heart the assistance it needs. It is worth emphasising here that the hardening of the arteries is specifically caused by nicotine, so isn't reduced by vaping instead of smoking for example. Tests have shown that the hardening of the arteries through vaping is virtually the same as for cigarette smoke.

Secondly high blood pressure can damage organs. After all, the blood isn't just flowing through your heart and arteries, it is ending up in organs which again can deal with a certain amount of pressure but not too much. Just to give some examples, high blood pressure can cause damage to blood vessels in the brain causing them to rupture or bleed (which is what is known as a stroke). It can cause damage to the blood vessels that supply blood to the eyes which can cause numerous issues including blindness. It can cause damage to tiny blood vessels in the kidneys, impairing their ability to filter waste from the blood.

So all in all high blood pressure is not a good thing.

At the other end of the scale low blood pressure is also bad. The effect is a bit simpler with low blood pressure and is simply that your organs (including crucially your brain) may not be getting enough oxygen because there is not enough oxygen carrying blood getting to them. Think of living in a house with several stories; if the water pressure drops the taps on your top floor are going to slow to a trickle and eventually stop.

Now we have the basics of blood pressure in place, let's look at how nicotine affects it.

Nicotine causes increases of up to 21 mm Hg in systolic blood pressure and 14 mm Hg in diastolic blood pressure. These spikes last for up to 30 minutes. In the long term this causes the health issues I've referred to above (hardening of the arteries which puts increasing pressure on your heart, increased risk of aneurism and stroke, and damage to organs) but the immediate, short term, effect is that you feel heavy and lethargic and lacking in energy.

When your blood pressure suddenly jumps up, your brain reacts. It knows that this spike in blood pressure is dangerous and potentially very damaging so it does all it can to bring your blood pressure down, and all it can do in respect of this is to stop you moving; after all moving around will put additional pressure on your heart and arteries as your heart rate increases to keep up with the increased demand for oxygen from your muscles.

Doesn't this mean that exercise is bad for you, if it increases your blood pressure? The answer is absolutely not. Exercise is natural, your body is designed to be active. As we have covered off above when talking about heart rate, regular exercise causes changes which means the heart can pump more blood with less effort. This in turn means that the force on the arteries decreases which causes an overall decrease in blood pressure.

So in this way nicotine makes you feel more alert and focussed mentally, but very heavy and lethargic physically. It also greatly increases your risk of various health issues. We often think of these detrimental health effects as a hit or miss affair; if you get one then bad luck, but if you don't then you get away with it. But this isn't the case. Things like heart attacks, stroke, aneurisms, cancer, and emphysema, only come about after a long-term weakening of the body that is caused by every single dose of nicotine you take.

Everyone knows that being unfit makes you far more likely to die younger, but fitness doesn't just have a huge impact on the length of your life, it also has a huge effect on the quality of it.

Exercise releases chemicals in the brain that make you feel positive, awake and happy. Fitness is associated with confidence, resilience and optimism. The reason for this is set in our genetic programming and linked with our survival instinct. When an animal is ill or injured, it needs to hide away, to rest, to give it the chance to recuperate and recover. However when it is well, when it is physically at its peak, it needs to be out there exploring, seeking food and mating. In this way our physical health and fitness is directly linked to our mental outlook. It isn't just 'illness' or 'wellness' that causes this, but our physical state generally. The fitter and stronger you are the more adventurous, positive and resilient you will feel. The erosion of our fitness and the feeling of lethargy that every dose of nicotine creates has a direct impact on our mental state. The problem is that the erosion of our fitness and the feeling of lethargy is accumulative; the more years we've been taking nicotine for the more pronounced the effect.

In short your body is the vehicle in which you travel through life. Would you rather be travelling in a clapped out banger, struggling along in first gear, always on the verge of stalling? Or would you rather be burning up the road in a Formula 1 car? Your body can either be a millstone around your neck, dragging you down, or it can be a powerful tool making you feel fit and capable and alive.

Every time you take a dose of nicotine you get a mental credit from the stimulating effect of the nicotine, but a corresponding physical debit. The debit on the physical side becomes increasingly more detrimental the more you consume, and even the mental credit actually (after a very short space of time) does no more than put you back where you would have been had you never started consuming nicotine in the first place. Let's now dissect and examine this last point in more detail.

3. The Mental Effects of Nicotine

So, as we've covered so far, nicotine is a stimulant so it gives us a mental boost. It leaves us feeling more awake and alert after we've taken it due to the stimulating effect of the nicotine on the brain. The problem is that the brain is not a passive object, it is reactive, and it reacts to regular doses of nicotine in such a way as to entirely negate any apparent benefit. To understand this concept fully we firstly need to obtain a basic understanding of the human brain and how it works.

The human brain creates and excretes its own store of naturally occurring drugs, hormones and chemicals. It also regulates how long these drugs, hormones and chemicals stay in our system for, and how we react to them. Human understanding of this is in its infancy, we do not even have a full list of all these drugs, hormones and chemicals, let alone do we understand how they all interact with one another. It is like a self-contained ecosystem, something that works by a delicate, intricate balance of all the different parts of it. For those not familiar with the concept, the introduction of rabbits to Australia is a good example. Rabbits are not indigenous to Australia and in 1788 rabbits were introduced from England. Since then they have devastated the environment, depleting vegetation which has led to the loss of numerous indigenous species.

This is why, when people are diagnosed with mental illness as a result of a chemical imbalance in the brain, the solution is rarely, if ever, straightforward. It is a process of trial and error involving close collaboration between the patient and the medical staff. Because our understanding of the chemical working of the human brain is so limited, introducing a drug to remedy a problem can have numerous unintended consequences.

Fortunately to understand the effects of nicotine on our mental state, we don't need to have a full and complete understanding of all the chemical processes of the human brain. We simply need to appreciate that the brain has a complicated array of its own chemicals, drugs and hormones, that these work in balance with one another, and if anything happens to upset this balance, the brain will seek to counter this in order to restore that balance.

Once we have this understanding in place, it is useful to cover off quickly the two main types of drugs. These are stimulants and depressants. Stimulants wake us up, increase our heart rate, and make us feel more alert. Our brain will release small amounts of these into our system when we wake up so that we feel awake and are ready to face the day. It will release larger amounts of these if we perceive a threat; the heart speeds up in anticipation of the increased physical activity that will be needed imminently (to either fight or run away), and this greater alertness gives us a better chance of dealing with the threat.

Depressants however depress, or inhibit nerve activity, making us feel relaxed and calm. Your brain increases the release of these when, for example, we are winding down to go to sleep.

The first time you take nicotine the nicotine will make you feel more alert and awake. The problem is that your brain recognises that you are over stimulated, so takes steps to counter this over stimulated effect. It does this by decreasing the amount of naturally occurring stimulants in your system. As the effect of the nicotine wears off, you feel less mentally alert then you did before you consumed it. The nicotine has worn off, but your own naturally occurring stimulants are now low. There is a chemical imbalance because your brain has recalibrated to work under the stimulating effects of the nicotine, but there is no nicotine present. This imbalance leaves us feeling anxious, out of sorts, easily overwhelmed, and slightly foggy. In short it is not a pleasant feeling. What do we do when we have an unpleasant feeling? We try to get rid of it. There are two very simple ways to get rid of the withdrawal from nicotine. One is to wait a few days for the chemical balance of your brain to return to normal. But who wants to feel unpleasant for a few days? We want to feel good now. (Un)fortunately there is a far quicker way to get rid of that unpleasant feeling, and that is to take another dose of nicotine. After all the unpleasant feeling exists because your brain is geared up to work under the stimulating effects of the nicotine but the nicotine has gone. Replacing the nicotine immediately replaces the chemical imbalance and makes you feel immediately better. In this way you need another dose of nicotine to get you back to where you need to be. The next dose does make you feel better and more alert, but you are actually no more alert than you would be had you never taken that first dose.

Think of those memory foam mattresses, the ones that mould to your exact shape when you lie on them. You lie down and to begin with you are lying on top of it, but slowly you begin to sink into it. When you eventually get up there is a 'you' shaped indent in the mattress, which slowly disappears after you get up and the mattress slowly reverts back to its original flat shape. When you took your first dose of nicotine you put a cigarette or vape or pouch onto the soft surface of your brain. Over time it has sunk into it, in much the same way as you would sink into that memory foam mattress. When the drug wears off it leaves a cigarette or vape or pouch shaped hole that creates a void that needs another cigarette or vape or pouch to fill it. Drugs are fleeting things, their effect never lasts long, they all too quickly run their course and leave your system. When this happens you are left with a hole, a void, that can only be filled by another cigarette or vape or pouch. It is a hole that didn't exist before you took that first dose of nicotine, and it is a hole that will very quickly disappear if you never take another dose again.

As I have mentioned, this period where the nicotine starts to wear off, leaving you with a chemical imbalance because you are now low on simulants, is the withdrawal period. It's not just a feeling of being less alert; the chemical imbalance has a far greater impact than just that. In the next chapter we will consider in detail the effect of this withdrawal.

4. Nicotine Withdrawal

As we have covered previously, nicotine is a chemical stimulant. When you take it your brain seeks to counter it, with the effect that when the nicotine wears off there is a chemical imbalance in the brain. This is the withdrawal period. It helps to visualise it with the following graphs.

This first graph is our natural, nicotine-free state. As you can see the stimulants and depressants are roughly equal. This balance means we are feeling good mentally: confident, resilient, and generally quite happy.

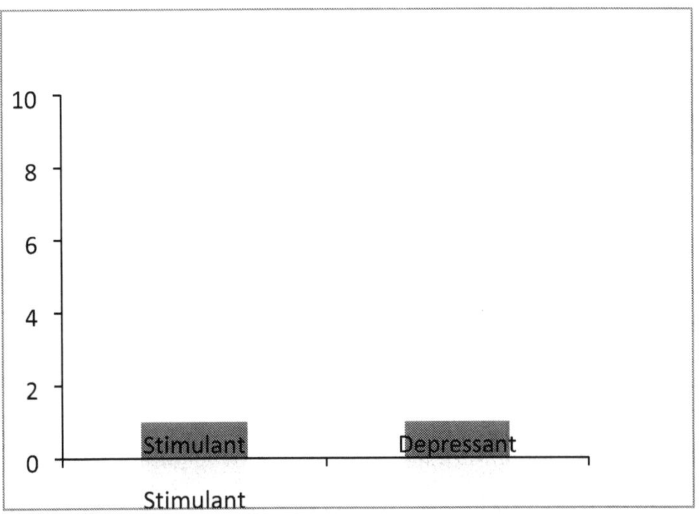

We than consume some nicotine. The results of this are shown in this second graph. As you can see the nicotine has a stimulating effect, leaving us mentally more awake and alert (although, as we have dealt with previously, it also leaves us feeling physically exhausted).

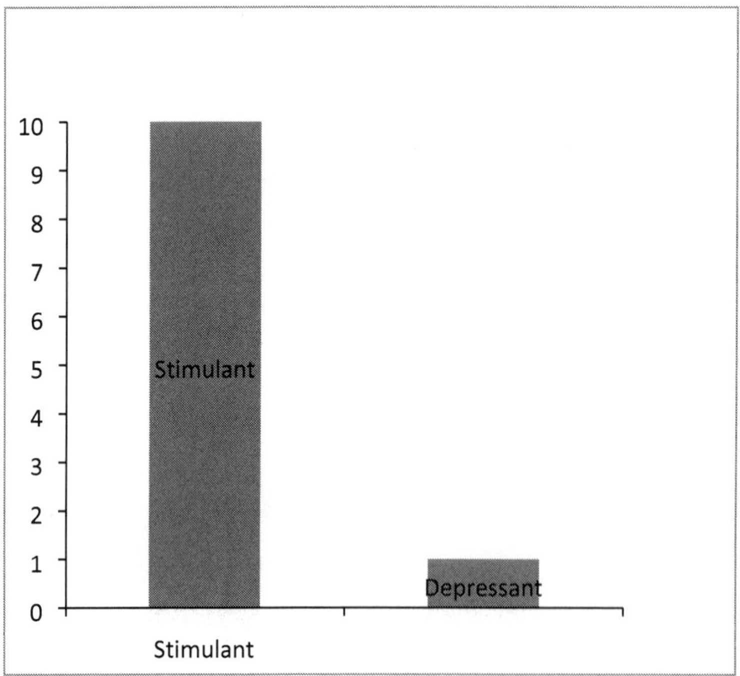

The brain looks to counter this overstimulation of the mind. The mechanics of this are complicated and not fully understood, but current indications are that some depressants are released, and some receptors that interpret the stimulating effects of both the nicotine and other naturally occurring stimulants temporarily cease working. For the purposes of understanding how nicotine withdrawal affects us the mechanism is less important than the effect, which is that the brain counters the overstimulation of the brain by increasing the depressant side of the scales. As you can see, when it does this, the stimulant / depressant values are more closely aligned.

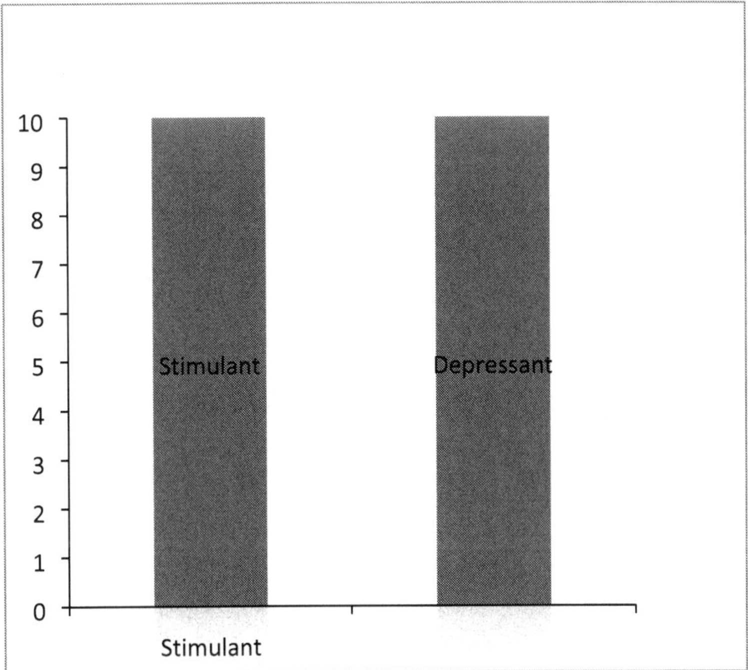

The nicotine then wears off, with the effect that the brain is then insufficiently stimulated, and there is now a chemical imbalance.

This is shown in the next graph and is essentially nicotine withdrawal.

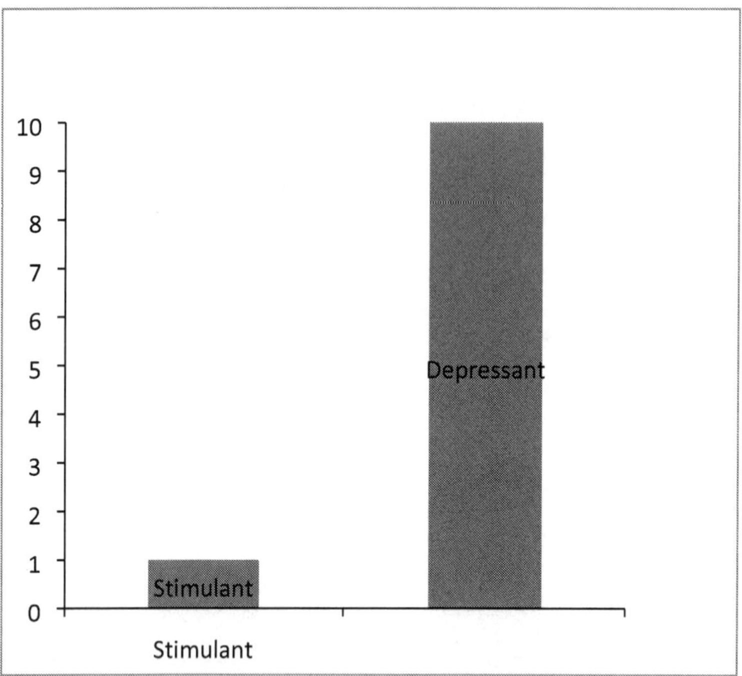

The quickest way to rectify this imbalance is to take another dose of nicotine, which brings the stimulant level back up and redresses the chemical imbalance caused by the previous dose.

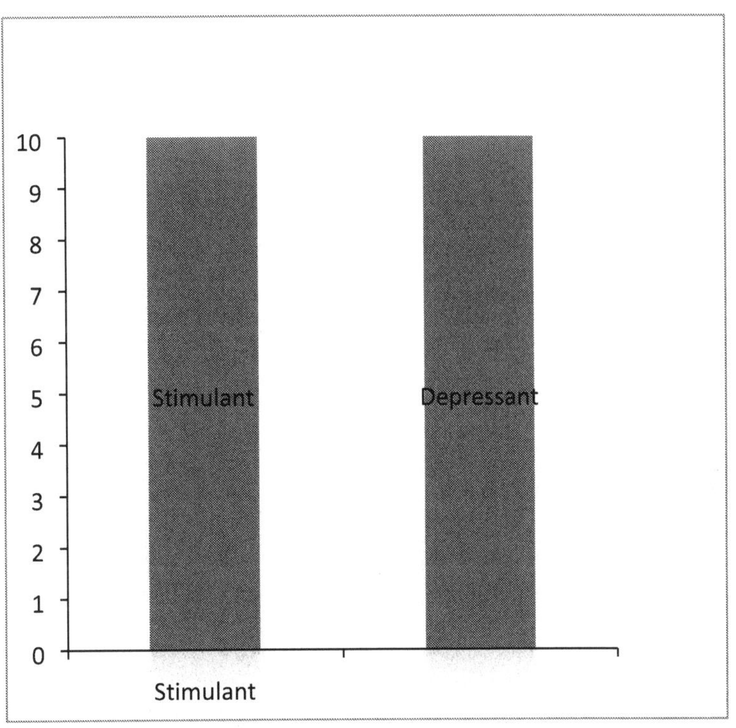

As mentioned previously, the nicotine withdrawal isn't just a case of feeling slightly dulled, it is far more invasive than that. The imbalance actually causes us to feel out of sorts, wary and nervous. It causes us to be timid; it is essentially a feeling of being less able to cope. A dose of nicotine, which then relieves that feeling, makes us feel courageous, happy, and able to cope with life. It is a subtle difference but a crucial one, but it is a feeling that essentially comes from having a good natural balance in our brains. It is a feeling we would have all the time had we not interfered with the chemical balance in our brains in the first place.

When people are consuming nicotine regularly they are either suffering the withdrawal or relieving it with a dose of nicotine. When they are in the withdrawal phase they feel slightly anxious and unable to cope. When they relieve the withdrawal (which they do by consuming nicotine) they feel content, confident and able to cope with and enjoy life. This is why people find it so hard to quit, and why they are prepared to incur horrendous disease and lose decades from their life span. It is simply that life in the withdrawal is unpleasant, and relieving the withdrawal makes life fun and liveable again. It is, quite literally, the difference between actually enjoying life, and simply suffering it. Given this, it is (on one level) a perfectly rational choice to continue to regularly take doses of nicotine despite the health problems it causes. Most people (myself included) would choose a shorter, enjoyable life, than a longer life with very little pleasure in it. Fortunately this apparent choice is pure illusion, it is entirely possible to have a longer and far more enjoyable life by quitting nicotine.

I have mentioned several times about how nicotine withdrawal actually feels; I've described it as feeling slightly woolly headed, unfocussed, anxious and timid. You may be thinking that this isn't right at all, that when you really want your dose of nicotine you almost feel panicked. This is because regularly consuming nicotine isn't simply a case of:

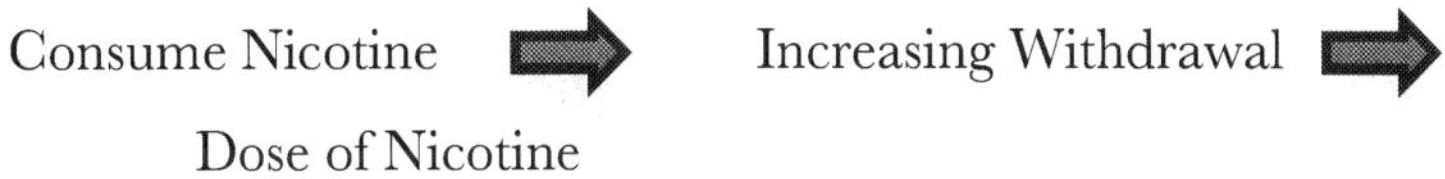

It is slightly more complicated than that because when you know you are about to take nicotine, there is often a physiological reaction that kicks in which heightens the withdrawal just before you take that dose. We will cover this fully in the next chapter.

5. The Physiological Effects of Anticipation

I used to sleep all night without consuming any nicotine. I would wake up feeling ok (or what I thought was ok; the heavy, lethargic feeling that came from regular consumption of nicotine was just part and parcel of my life, so I took it as normal not realising how much it had already dragged me down). But when I sat down to smoke my first cigarette of the day, or put the first pouch of the day in my mouth, I could feel my heart start to speed up BEFORE I HAD EVEN LIT THE CIGARETTE, OR BEFORE THE POUCH WAS EVEN IN MY MOUTH.

I would also notice this tendency when I woke up with no nicotine in the house (usually because I was trying to give up). After the usual mental toing and froing, and eventually deciding that I was allowed some nicotine (because this was a particularly bad time for whatever reason, and that tomorrow / next week / next month etc was a far better time to quit) my heart rate would increase dramatically and I would literally be in a panic to get that nicotine inside me. I would walk to the shop at roughly the same pace as Usain Bolt competing in the 100 metres, and would stand in the queue with my heart hammering, internally screaming as the person in front of me counted out their payment in pennies.

The point here is that when I knew I would be consuming nicotine, there was an actual physiological effect that happened even before any of that nicotine hit my bloodstream.

This process is well documented in similar situations; human beings react in much the same way to an imaginary event as a real one. For example fear causes your brain to release adrenaline, it doesn't matter if the source of the fear is real or imagined. If you have ever watched a horror film and jumped out of your skin you will know exactly what I am talking about. The human imagination is a great thing; when we lose ourselves in the moment, when we forget everything that is going on apart from the story such that we become part of it, our brain and body reacts as if we were really there.

Think back to the basic physiological effect of taking nicotine. Our brain seeks to counter the effects by creating a cigarette or vape or pouch shaped hole so that when we take the drug our brain can work normally even under the stimulating effect of the drug. It is complete and normal only with the drug. But remember also that over a short period of time without the drug, our brain goes back to normal. Think about that memory foam mattress that has a 'you' shaped imprint in it when you get up in the morning, but slowly goes back to its original flat shape after you get up.

The analogy with the mattress is a good one, but it has one failing; the mattress can only react, it cannot anticipate, whereas the brain can. The mattress is flat until you lay on it, then it slowly gives way to your precise shape, but the brain can anticipate and take steps. After all, your brain needs to make changes to counter the stimulating effects of the nicotine. Why should it wait until you actually have nicotine coursing through your veins? Why would it not start to accommodate the nicotine before you actually take it?

When you make an absolute decision to take nicotine, and you know that you will be consuming nicotine imminently, your brain starts the recalibration process. Imagine a memory foam mattress that knows when you are about to go to bed, so starts to create a 'you' shaped indent before you even lie down. This is how the desire for nicotine can sharpen and become almost unbearable just before you actually consume it.

Sometimes I would wake up having been in bed for 8 hours, shower and commute into the City of London before having my first dose of nicotine. I could go for ten hours or more without a dose of nicotine and although I might not have been at my most content and relaxed, it was entirely bearable. But when I had sat down to actually take that dose of nicotine, if that nicotine had been snatched away from me at that point, it would have been unbearable.

When you decide that you are going to end up taking a dose of nicotine, this has an actual, physical effect. Your brain starts to recalibrate in anticipation of the nicotine and the desire / need becomes acute. At this point you are almost in a panic to get that dose of nicotine inside you.

This panic feeling is often considered to be part of the withdrawal, but it isn't; it is the anticipation and the refinement of the physical desire that comes as a result of that.

Some people when they stop nicotine describe it as hell, others will say something like 'it was surprisingly easy once I put my mind to it'. The reason for this disparity is because if you know at a fairly deep level that that you aren't going to consume nicotine again, then you can completely bypass two of the biggest hurdles in quitting: the craving (which I will deal with in the next chapter) and that panic feeling, that acute desire, that is a result of your brain acclimatising to an imminent dose of nicotine.

So how can you know that you will never use nicotine again? If you are anything like me you will have made the promise to quit and broken it more times than you can remember. Also we are talking about something quite deep here. We have to KNOW that we will never consume nicotine again. But how can we ever know when we have got to that stage?

In fact the best way to get to that stage is to not even worry about it. You are more likely to get to that stage if you concentrate on re-evaluating nicotine, your reasons for taking it, and how much better your life will be without it. Distracting yourself with how deep the knowledge has gone can be counter productive. If this is the case why did I mention it? Firstly because this book is about explaining nicotine addiction, and this is a key element of it. Secondly you need to understand all the elements of what you may encounter when you quit, and a full explanation of these.

The other reason that it is best not to worry about it is that different people learn in different ways. Some people learn best from academic theory, other people learn best from practical experience. The vast majority of people need a bit of both, but most will favour one over the other.

If you learn well by theory, and if I have done my job properly in writing this book, then by the end of it you may well find that you know that you aren't going to take nicotine again, come what may.

On the other hand you may learn better by practical application, or my writing style may not quite hit the mark with you or may even grate on you. In this case you may finish the book and need time to mull things over, to see how things tally with your own experience, and so it may take time.

It's worth remembering that many many people do quit the hard way. They sit and they suffer, they torture themselves and get into that panicked state because they want that dose of nicotine so badly. Yet still they don't give in. And slowly, slowly, they adjust to a life without nicotine. They end up going out for drinks, meals and social occasions. They wake up in the morning and enjoy a cup of coffee. In short, they learn through practical experience what I am trying to explain in this book; that there is life after nicotine, and contrary to popular belief it is a far far better life than that experienced by the regular nicotine consumer. If we can remove even some of these difficulties then we are already better off.

It is also worth thinking about it this way. The point of this book is to encourage you to make an attempt to quit nicotine, and to make it as easy as possible so you have the best chance of succeeding. I cannot know what you are paying for your nicotine, but here in the UK this book is on sale for way less than a packet of cigarettes, a tub of pouches, or a vape. Quit for a single day and you've most likely made back the money you spent on this book. Quit for two days and you've doubled your money. Quit for a week, a month, a year, and you'll have made one of the best returns on an investment that you've ever made, and that's just the financial side of things; it doesn't even account for the longer, better quality, happier life you'll lead.

Let's assume that the average smoker is going to suffer from regular intense physical cravings when they quit nicotine for 4 weeks after they quit. If this book (or indeed any other book or any other method of quitting) can remove all of these then that is fantastic. But even if it can remove half or even a quarter of these, then that is still good. Even if it just removes one of them, or even if it fails to remove one of them, it's still worth doing if it ends up with you quitting.

The point is that certainty will make the process easier. Some people will be certain from the moment they quit (or even before that), for others it may take a bit of time and practical experience to achieve that certainty. Some people may be certain one day, then uncertain the next. It is impossible to know what your personal experience will be, but the best way to make it as easy as possible is to focus on not consuming nicotine. Don't get hung up on how certain you are or not, just know that you aren't going to consume nicotine, come what may. Whether it is easy or hard, whether you crave or not, whether you get that panic feeling or not, you just aren't going to take nicotine ever again.

For 6 years of my life I was in the 4th Battalion of the Parachute Regiment, which is the reserve battalion (which means I held down a civilian job and did military training in the evenings and weekends). I served out in in Iraq for 6 months from 2005 – 2006. Coming back to civilian life was hard, mainly because in the military (and particularly in the Parachute Regiment) things get done. There is a different approach to civilian life. In my civilian job, if you ask someone to do something, half the time they come back to you to explain why they couldn't do it. These reasons may be valid and sensible, but the bottom line is the task doesn't get done. In the military things were different; if you got told to do something it got done. You may have to blow up a building, wreck a vehicle, or lose a leg in the process, but it got done.

I was sent a meme once that showed a mouse in a maze. The entrance to the maze was at one side, and the piece of cheese was at the other. The mouse was happily eating the cheese, and between it and the entrance to the maze every wall had been demolished. The writing around the top of the picture was 'Paratrooper Mentality'.

When you quit nicotine you are the mouse and the piece of cheese is quitting nicotine. The walls to the maze are all the reasons you might want to take nicotine again: 'now is not a good time to quit', 'just this once', 'you've got to have some pleasure in life'. The walls are seeing other people taking nicotine, it is waking up in the morning and missing that dose, it is having a tough day ahead and feeling like you just need something to get you through it. You need to bulldoze through all of those walls to get to that piece of cheese. The mindset should not be 'I need to quit nicotine but look at all these difficulties, these situations I will struggle in', it has to be 'I am quitting nicotine no matter what, anything and everything else is going to have to fall into place around that.'

Just remember that no one can make you take nicotine. It is your decision, and your decision alone. Even if you have the worst experience possible, there is no physical pain. Wanting something you can't have may not feel pleasant, but compared to all the horrors that are currently going on in the world, it is comparatively insignificant. You need to make sure that your mind-set is 'I am not going to take nicotine no matter what'. Don't allow your course to be dictated by the walls of the maze.

If you do end up in that panic to get some nicotine into your bloodstream, then stop for a moment and try to clear your mind. Pause, empty your mind for a moment, and ask yourself where this terrible feeling is. Where is this great pain of withdrawal? There is no physical pain. At the most it can be described as unpleasant, but it is not physically painful.

I mentioned in this chapter that certainty can mean you avoid this physiological effect of anticipation, but also that it can mean you avoid craving. You may well be wondering how anything can stop you craving nicotine. Let's now cover off this all important topic, that of craving.

6. Craving

Craving, or an intense desire for something, is a major part of addiction. Most definitions of addiction will include craving. But what actually is a craving?

People often think of craving as something external that happens to us, like getting a cold. They think that when you start craving you have a choice of two alternatives: suffer the craving or give in to it. But actually, cravings are not an external occurrence that affect us, they are an entirely conscious thought process. This means that a craving is the result of a specific chain of thoughts and, unlike the subconscious triggers (which I deal with in a later chapter), this thought process occurs entirely in our conscious mind.

The craving cycle is often put in process by the physical withdrawal. As soon as you finish a dose of nicotine, the nicotine starts to leave your system and over time you start to feel more and more out of sorts. You start to feel slightly woolly headed, slightly groggy, clarity of thought and mental resilience slowly ebbs away and your confidence starts to erode. Your brain has learned, through cause and effect from every one of the many thousands of doses that you have consumed over the course of your life, that another dose will remedy this unpleasant feeling. This process actually takes place in your subconscious mind, which means a part of your brain that triggers reactions without you being consciously aware of it – this is covered off in detail in a later chapter. So your brain triggers the thought of reaching for that next dose.

So now you feel out of kilter and you know that another dose will take away that unpleasant feeling and get you back to that wonderful feeling of clarity and confidence that non-nicotine addicts experience all the time. This is where the mental process of craving begins.

In terms of actual physical pain, the withdrawal from nicotine rates nowhere; there is no physical pain. It is unpleasant, but even then it is not particularly significant. It is most similar to that woolly headedness and slight disorientation that you get when you have a cold or if you skip your morning coffee one morning. However when you start to get that feeling, the brain triggers the thought of having a dose of nicotine and if for any reason you can't have one, the usual thing to do is to start to fantasise about it. If you are a smoker you imagine taking the cigarette from the packet, the firm crackly feel of it, the smell of the tobacco. You think about putting it in your mouth, of lighting it, of drawing the smoke into your lungs, and that wonderful feeling of clarity and confidence that it brings. Or if you are a vaper then you think about your vape, and the hit you get when the nicotine laden vapour hits your lungs and enters your bloodstream (or the pouch or whatever your chosen method of consuming nicotine is).

This is, in essence, what a craving is. It is FANTASISING about something. It is teasing yourself with the thought of it, like being really hungry and sitting there staring at your favourite food and not being allowed to eat it. The problem is that when you start doing that you are no longer concentrating on whatever else it was you were doing at the time. If you are at work you can't concentrate on the job in hand, if you are out socialising you are no longer paying any attention to anything anyone is saying to you, if you are at home (supposedly) relaxing you are suddenly tense and unable to relax. Whatever it is you are supposed to be doing, you are no longer engaged in it, your mind is elsewhere, fantasising about how wonderful it would be if only you could take that dose of nicotine.

All things being equal this craving process just goes on indefinitely. Your life quite literally goes on hold while you torture yourself with the thought of how good it would feel to get that poison inside you, and how miserable you are because you can't. This is really why nicotine and indeed any drug can have such a strong hold on people; it really is the difference between living and enjoying life, and sitting there miserable just waiting for time to pass. This is in essence why people continue to take nicotine despite the drastically reduced lifespan and all the other issues that it causes them. As they see it, they have a choice of a long pointless grey life with no joy or colour in it, or a shorter life with some actual pleasure in it. In fact this choice of two is false, all the supposed pleasure of nicotine can be obtained by simply stopping for a few days; the clarity of mind, the confidence and mental resilience, indeed all the benefits of that next dose of nicotine and more can be obtained by simply allowing your brain to return to normal. As the brain gets back on an even keel you have all the benefits of nicotine without actually having to consume any and as your fitness returns, so will you feel more confident and resilient than you ever did as a regular consumer of nicotine.

The craving process also explains why sometimes we can go for some quite extended periods without nicotine, and sometimes we simply can't. Nicotine consumers can go several hours while sleeping at night without nicotine and the desire for it doesn't even wake them up. However they could not last a fraction of that time if they were out drinking with friends, or socialising, or having their first cup of tea or coffee of the day, or whatever the situation is in which they usually take a dose. Nicotine consumers can get on planes or trains, go to the cinema or theatre, and in fact do numerous things without climbing up the wall for a dose but when they start to crave, the desire becomes virtually irresistible. The physical withdrawal side may be exactly the same, but the differentiating factor is whether or not the craving, the mental torture, is underway.

One of the main reasons that regular consumers of nicotine can go without nicotine (sometimes for some quite extended periods) and not crave is certainty. If you smoke or vape and you are on a plane and know you cannot take that dose, come what may, you are less likely to waste time thinking about it. Compare this to waking up a couple of days into an attempt to quit, when the withdrawal is in full swing, and you start to question your decision to stop. When you are weighing up whether to do or not do something, you weigh up the pros and cons. How do you weigh up the pro side of nicotine? Well that's easy to do, just think about how it would feel if you were take a dose. That is in essence the start of the craving process; it is running through in your mind how it would really feel to consume that dose of nicotine.

Although the craving process is extremely powerful, it is fortunately something that takes place entirely in the conscious mind and is therefore entirely in our control.

In fact it is actually possible to break the craving process down into its constituent phases to help us understand it more fully. There are actually 5 stages in the craving process that I have identified:

1. **The Thought of Nicotine**

   The first stage of the process is when the thought of having nicotine enters into our head. This is not actually part of the craving process, but it is always the start of it. By this I mean that it is possible to think about nicotine without actually craving it. Take me for example, while writing this book I have been thinking about nicotine probably 90% of my waking hours, but I have never once craved it. Why is that? It is because although I am thinking about nicotine, I am thinking about it on an academic level, I never entertain the thought of actually having any. If I were to do this then I would enter into the next stage of the process which is…

2. **Fantasising**

   When the thought of nicotine enters my mind, I always think about how lucky I am to be free. I remember the heavy, drained feeling, the worry about being ensnared or trapped, the health impact, the cost, and how feeling the buzz would be compared to then having hours of repeated doses just to feel normal (again I deal with this aspect in more detail in a later chapter). In short, I remind myself how glad I am to be free and how much better my life is now I've quit. What I don't do is start fantasising about it, thinking about how good it would feel to have a hit of nicotine, because if I started doing this I would very quickly move onto the next stage of the craving process which is…

3. **Considering the Possibility**

   This is where we start to think about the possibility of having some nicotine. We move from fantasising about it, to considering the actual possibility of having some. This sharpens the torture as the anticipation starts and becomes increasingly more acute. Imagine being really hungry and thinking about your favourite food. This wouldn't be a particularly pleasant thing to do, but if you then had some of that food in front of you, so you could smell it, almost taste it, the torture would be even more acute. If we are trying to quit, this is where we start to think things like 'maybe now isn't the best time', 'next week / month / year will be a far better time to quit', and 'maybe I could have just one on this one occasion'.

4. **Subconscious Decision Making**

   There have been numerous psychological studies to show that often human decision-making is a process handled to a large extent by a subconscious part of our brain. Often decisions are made subconsciously before we consciously make the decision. In this situation the subconscious has made the decision, and your conscious mind isn't actually making a decision (that is already done), rather it is looking to justify that decision. It is a process I call…

5. **The Search for Excuses**

   When you hit this stage you are going to consume nicotine, that decision has already been made, but your conscious mind has yet to catch up. At this point your thinking shifts slightly; you are no longer rationally considering something, rather you are looking to justify it. There may be a thousand good reasons to never take

> nicotine again, and only a few flimsy reasons to have just one more dose. Because at this stage we are actually searching for an excuse to do something we have already decided to do, we deliberately ignore all the reasons we should stop, and only consider any reason why we might want to carry on. We quickly sift through all the thoughts we have about nicotine. If it's a sensible reason to quit, we discard it. If it's one of our flimsy excuses to carry on, we hold onto it. Humans can only think of a limited number of things at any one time (usually estimated at around 7). We may have a thousand reasons to quit, and only ten justifying taking that next dose, but if we can hold onto 7 of those ten reasons then our mind is full of reasons to take the dose, and no reasons not to. At this point we've 'justified' our decision, so run full pelt to that next dose of nicotine and get it inside us before we have to change our minds again.

The problem is with this process that (as we've covered previously) when the subconscious decides you are going to end up taking a dose of nicotine, this has an actual, physical effect. Your brain starts to recalibrate in anticipation of the nicotine and the desire / need becomes acute. At this point you are almost in a panic to get that dose of nicotine inside you.

To recap, this again is why certainty is key. When you quit nicotine you will think about it at some point. There is an awful lot of nicotine in the world, and an awful lot of people consuming it, so it is only a matter of time before you come across it. Not only that but there will be many situations in your life when you would previously have had some nicotine, and when you encounter these after you have quit you will naturally think about nicotine. So you will be thinking about nicotine at some point.

If you know, absolutely 100% know, that you aren't going to consume nicotine again then when the thought of a cigarette or vape or pouch enters your mind you won't start fantasising about it and you certainly won't seriously consider actually consuming any. You may, like me, think about nicotine on an academic level but you will not start fantasising about taking it and you will certainly not start considering the possibility of consuming some. There will be no subconscious or conscious decision to take nicotine and so no physiological refinement of the desire and so no deep panic. This is how some people manage to quit with no cravings, no panic, and no agony. There is just a short period of feeling slightly out of sorts until their brain readjusts.

Look again at the 5 parts of craving I have identified above. The best way to disrupt the process is between parts 1 and 2. When the thought of nicotine enters your mind, there are two ways that thought can go. It can move on to part 2 of the craving process and then through to the end, or you can divert the thought elsewhere. If every time the thought of nicotine enters your mind you use it as a chance to congratulate yourself on the fact that you are now free, to remember:

- that heavy, drained feeling that nicotine produces in you and be thankful that you never have to experience it again,

- that you are now finally free of all the years when you were forced against your will to keep taking something that you really wanted to be free of

- that now you are fitter, stronger, more mentally resilient,

- that you are no longer throwing money away on a poison,

then you won't move on to stage 2 at all. You will entirely divert your thoughts away from the craving process.

If you do end up craving then you can still divert your mind from the process at any point, although it does take more effort as you need to completely disengage from the thought process of craving. I will cover off tactics for diverting your mind from the craving process towards the end of the book.

7. Do We Enjoy Consuming Nicotine?

Think about the dynamic of making an attempt to quit and then failing. You stop, the withdrawal builds up, you start to crave and obsess, very soon you are between a rock and a hard place. On the one hand you desperately want to quit, on the other hand you desperately want a dose of nicotine so that you can feel better and can get on with your life.

So what happens if you do give in and consume some nicotine? After all, this is in many ways the crucial point if you are trying to quit. It's what keeps pulling us in, despite all our good intentions to quit. It's important that we cover this off so you understand exactly what is at stake. We have covered off a lot of this before but it is very useful to consolidate this into the actual user experience.

You finish the day having consumed your usual amount of nicotine. You feel lethargic and you have that residual feeling of anxiety (which is the usual state of the habitual nicotine consumer and is covered in more detail in a later chapter). You don't like it. You know you'd be better off without it. So you tell yourself that now is the time to quit.

The problem is that when you wake up the next day, virtually all the nicotine has left your system. You are in withdrawal. Minor stresses and strains of everyday life start to feel overpowering. Of course you think about having that cigarette, or vape, or pouch. You start to obsess about it, to crave. You want it, but you also want to quit. You find you can't focus on anything else. You know that if you just have the damn thing you won't be obsessing about it and you can just get on with your day. You go through the whole 'now is not the right time' debacle. You start the 'search for excuses'. You tell yourself that tomorrow, or next week, or next month, or next year will be the best time to quit. So you buy your nicotine and go ahead and consume it.

The immediate effect is lovely. The craving ends, you feel more alert, more focussed, more confident and resilient, more enthusiastic, more able to cope with all those annoyances that seemed so overpowering. The problem though is twofold.

Firstly, this wonderful feeling only lasts for a few minutes (4 or 5 at most). After that it's gone for the day (unless you have to go for an extended period during the day without any nicotine). Another dose of nicotine now won't give you that wonderful feeling, because you already have nicotine flowing through your veins. You only get that feeling when you consume a dose of nicotine after a substantial period of abstinence. That wonderful feeling is no more than just returning to normal and now, with the nicotine flowing through your veins, you are closer to normal than you were before. Every other dose for the rest of the day won't do much of anything.

Secondly you will find that after that initial 'buzz' you feel heavy and lethargic. In short you feel how you do your whole life as a regular nicotine consumer; physically you feel a bit heavy and lacking in energy, mentally you may feel ok from a physiological perspective (in that you no longer feel quite so sluggish), but psychologically you feel worse, because once again you've failed to quit. That momentary lift is gone and once again it's all been for nothing. You're back where you started. We try to temper this by telling ourselves that we will quit, and next time it will be different. This thought gives us some comfort, but the more times we don't quit, the more times we give in, the harder it is to convince ourselves that this is true. The more times you do this the more helpless and trapped you feel. The more times you fail to quit, the more you have to accept that you are not in control, that you are addicted. So you get a very short, superficial lift, followed by a long term quite pronounced detriment in the form of a greatly reduced quality of life, both physical and psychological.

When you quit, and you want that dose of nicotine, you might not feel great. Let's say you're 20 points below par. You feel a bit out of sorts and you want that lovely focussed feeling a dose of nicotine will give you. If you take that dose of nicotine you may then find you are 5 points above par, so you get a 25 point boost. But that boost is very short lived, and you very quickly drop to being 20 points below par or even more. That heavy feeling, the feeling of failure, the feeling of being ensnared and unable to escape, very quickly makes you feel well below par again. In short you will feel just as bad, or even worse, just for different reasons. This is something to keep very firmly in your mind when you quit. The only true and complete way to feel truly good again is to wait a few days and to come out the other side of the withdrawal.

Also keep in mind that this wonderful feeling, this 'buzz', is nothing more than how you would feel all the time after just a few days had you just kept to your resolution to quit the nicotine once and for all.

8. Hunger

Whether you believe we were created by God (in whatever form), you believe we are a result of the process of natural selection, or you believe in a combination of the two, it is a fact of our lives (and the lives all of living organisms on the planet) that we have certain driving forces that are designed to keep us alive and ensure our survival and the survival of our species. One of these driving forces that we encounter most regularly is hunger.

We don't tend to think of hunger as something we learn. In one sense this is correct, hunger is a physiological reaction caused by a lack of readily available energy and nutrients. In this sense then it is not something we learn. However in another sense hunger is learned in that what we hunger for is something we do learn and can change. Very few, if any, living creatures on the planet have such a reliable food source that it can be guaranteed that that food source can never run out. A species that was unable to adapt its diet in times when its usual food source runs low would not last long. So we have an innate ability to adapt our diet in times of need.

So how does this work? The hungrier you get the more desperate you get, and that desperation will cause you to eat whatever is available. When I talk about hunger here, I am talking about the kind of hunger that most of us living in a western society will, fortunately, never experience. I am talking about going for days, weeks or even months either without food entirely or with very little to eat.

When people or animals are starving their desperation will lead them to eat virtually anything: insects, rotten food, uncooked dead animals, any unfamiliar and untested fruits or berries. When they do this, one of two things will happen; either what they consumed was bad for them, in which case they will feel worse after they have eaten it, or it will have some kind of nutritional benefit, in which case they will feel better shortly after eating it.

When we are hungry eating will make us feel better, both physically and mentally. So if we consume something that we wouldn't usually hunger for, or something that tastes or smells offensive, and we feel immediately better after we consume it, the brain will conclude that what we immediately identified as poison actually had some form of nutritional benefit, i.e. that it is 'food' rather than 'poison', and as it didn't seem to harm us we can continue to consume it. As such and over time, we will cease to be repulsed by the smell and taste of it, instead, we will start to find it appetising and will start to hunger for it. In this way if a living creature's food source becomes scarce or disappears, they will be able to adapt to other food types through trial and error.

This is essentially what an 'acquired taste' is. If you take something that you find repulsive, but it appears to convey a benefit, you will learn to enjoy it. It is simply your brain reassessing what is 'repulsive' (i.e. bad for you) and what is tasty (i.e. good for you). When we first drink or smoke we can find the taste repulsive. That is your body correctly identifying it as a poison. It is your body telling you that it is bad for you and that you should stay away from it. However when the effect of the drug kicks in the brain starts to reassess things. It (incorrectly) concludes that what it initially identified as a poison is in fact beneficial, because it senses a benefit from having consumed it. Drugs confuse the system because they are poisons, but the effect of the drug is to make us feel 'better' (alcohol makes us feel more relaxed, nicotine makes us feel more alert) so the brain identifies it as beneficial rather than poisonous.

It is an amazing and incredible mechanism and has allowed many species to survive and thrive as they time and again adapt to changes in their environment. As we grow hungrier, we become more desperate and will eat a wider and wider variety of things. If we chance upon something that is actually good for us, we can adapt to it. If we poison ourselves in the process? Well, if we're in the process of starving to death anyway it scarcely makes much difference. It's an amazing process, however it has one main fatal flaw; it can be tricked by drugs.

The whole point of this phenomenon is that if we do something and it is good for us, we want to continue doing it. How do we know if something is good for us? Because it makes us feel better. The problem with drugs is that they make us feel better, but actually poison us. Nicotine makes us feel more awake, but not because it has actually done anything beneficial for us, but because we've introduced a drug that changes how we feel. Your brain concludes that you've had something invigorating and nourishing, in fact all that has happened is that it has interfered with your brains chemical balance making you feel like you've done something beneficial when in fact you've done the complete opposite.

A significant part of this process takes place in our subconscious mind, by this I mean that animals and humans alike don't consciously decide to train themselves to like certain flavours or experiences that they initially found unpleasant. It is a process that happens without us being consciously aware of it. This subconscious part of our brain has a huge impact on addiction generally and we are going to look at this in detail in the next chapter.

9. The Subconscious

The term 'subconscious' is bandied about quite a lot these days. It's often used to refer to anything that we do that we can't justify on a purely rational basis. I am using it in a far more restrictive sense. When I use the term I am referring to that part of our brain that automates certain actions and reactions.

A lot of our automated (i.e. non-conscious) responses are inherent (meaning we are born with them). Blinking when something flicks towards our eyes is one example of this. We don't learn this, we simply do it. However, as mentioned previously, all living things need to adapt to changes in their environment. It is therefore possible to learn instinctive behaviour. This happens when something is repeated over and over again, and confers an apparent benefit. In essence, when an action is repeated over and over again and provides the same results, the subconscious part of the brain learns that the action causes the result, and when that result is required, your brain automatically triggers the action required to obtain that result. 'Automatically' in this context means it is not a conscious decision, it is automated. The most obvious example of this is driving.

When you drive, you extend your right leg to slow down the vehicle you are driving. Every time you extend your right leg, the vehicle slows down. This is repeated over and over and over again for however many years you have been driving. The subconscious part of your brain learns that extending your right leg will slow down a vehicle, and it triggers this any time you are in a vehicle that is travelling too fast. This is why, if you are a passenger in a vehicle that is travelling too fast and / or driving too close to the vehicle in front, you will find your right leg will keep tensing up. There is no logical reason for this as there is no brake for a passenger in a vehicle, and this reaction is not in our genes (no one is born with this reaction). It is learned instinctive behaviour.

It is an amazing survival mechanism. No matter how your environment changes, within a short space of time the things you need to do to survive become automated, saving precious seconds. Again the flaw in the process is that it can be tricked by drugs.

The subconscious learns by cause and effect. In our driving example the cause is the extending of the right leg, the effect is the slowing down of the vehicle. With nicotine, the cause is whatever method of consuming nicotine that you favour (inhaling smoke or vapour, or absorbing it through your skin or gums), and the effect is when it hits your bloodstream (because the effects of a drug are felt when it enters your bloodstream).

Let's go back briefly to the physiological side of things for a moment. You take a dose of nicotine, and it wears off leaving an unpleasant feeling; a cigarette or vape or dip / snus shaped void. You can get rid of this unpleasant feeling, this void, in two ways. The slow, thorough way is to wait a few days for your brain chemistry to get back to normal. The quicker but entirely superficial way is to take another dose of the drug. This state of habitually taking a drug in order to relieve the withdrawal of the previous dose is what many people would think of as classic addicted behaviour, but this isn't necessarily the case.

Some people (particularly when in the very early stages of their nicotine career) may just consume nicotine on odd occasions without having to take it all day every day. I myself started smoking when out with my friends at the weekend, and for quite some time this is all I did. I would smoke at the weekend then not smoke all week. Some people only smoke when they drink, or vape when out with friends, so how does this fit in with what we know about nicotine (that is causes an unpleasant feeling or void that needs another dose to relieve it)?

Withdrawal from nicotine leaves us feeling out of sorts and not quite with it. It is not a pleasant feeling. But there are lots of times in our lives when we may feel unpleasant: an argument with our partner or friend or family, problems at work, an unexpected bill, the car breaking down or a problem with our house or flat. And what do we do when we feel bad? Well, most of the time we just get on with it. We get up, we go to work, in short we just carry on. This is what happens when we first start consuming nicotine; the withdrawal is there but we just ignore it and get on with our lives.

However over time the subconscious steps in. It starts to notice cause and effect (which is, after all, its purpose). It notices that there is a particular bad feeling that starts to accumulate after you finish a dose of nicotine, and this particular bad feeling can be relieved by another dose. As this formula of withdrawal and relief is repeated over and over, the subconscious triggers the desire for the next dose when the last dose starts wearing off. In this way each dose causes the desire for the next.

This is learned behaviour, and what is learned cannot be unlearned. Imagine that you have never encountered even the concept of maths before. I could explain the concept of numbering and basic addition and that 2 + 2 = 4. I could teach you that, but I could never 'unteach' you. When you learnt it, it would be in your brain forever. This is one of the reasons that, although we may have been able to take it or leave it with nicotine in the early stages of our relationship with it, when we start to take it regularly, we can never comfortably go back to that early state of only having it on certain occasions.

This is a key point; there is no reset with addiction. You may quit nicotine for a day, a month, a year, a decade, or 50 years, but if you ever take a dose of it again it will wear off leaving an unpleasant feeling and a part of your brain will jump in and say 'I remember this feeling, and I know just how to get rid of it. Just take another dose'.

Nicotine is not like food. If you want a certain type of food, and you eat it, you remove the desire for it. Nicotine is not like that. It is not food, but a drug. No matter how much of it you take, when it wears off you will want more.

The trouble is that you start to automatically reach for a dose of nicotine every time the withdrawal starts to build up. Remember, the withdrawal that is being relieved is a feeling of being out of sorts, a bit anxious and unable to cope, so you very soon find yourself reaching for a dose of nicotine every time you feel stressed, nervous, or upset. This is the case whether these feelings have been caused by the withdrawal or not, as your subconscious can't differentiate between the two.

This is why we associate nicotine with relaxation and confidence, and why the thought of never taking nicotine again causes us such consternation. What we are mainly concerned with when we contemplate stopping nicotine is how we will deal with those difficult situations that crop up. The fact of the matter is though that nicotine can never assist or relieve any genuine stress or upset, it can only relieve the additional stress caused by the withdrawal. Again it helps to visualise this with reference to some simple graphs.

Let's assume you have an argument with your partner, or have a problem at work, or whatever else would usually trigger you to want a dose of nicotine. In the graph below we can see our stress level. The grey is the genuine stress causes by the event in question; the black is the additional stress we are suffering due to the withdrawal.

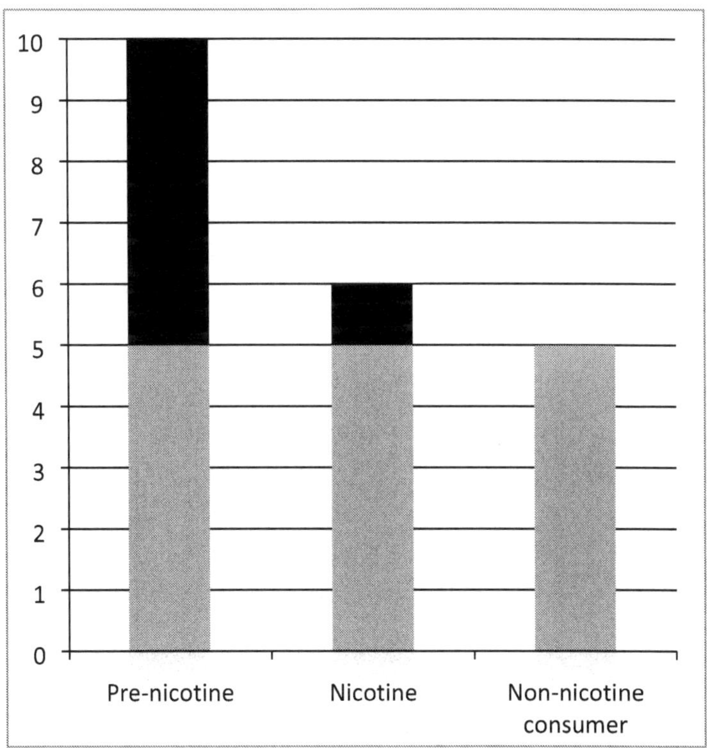

As you can see in the first column is the moment before we take a dose of nicotine. We are suffering ten points of stress, five from the event and five from the withdrawal. We cannot differentiate between the two, all we know is we are stressed and we put all the stress down to the event in question.

The second column is when we consume nicotine. As you can see, the overall stress is substantially reduced. Again, we cannot differentiate between the stress due to the event, and the stress due to the withdrawal. All we know is that the stress has been substantially reduced. The nicotine therefore seems to have eased the situation dramatically. In fact all it has done is exaggerated the problem by adding additional stress, and then has partially relieved that additional stress. You will note that there is still an element of withdrawal stress in this middle column. This is firstly because nicotine is a stimulant and the more you take of it the more anxious you feel. It's the same as when you drink too much coffee (this concept is dealt with in more detail in a later chapter). Secondly remember that nicotine erodes your fitness and therefore your confidence and optimism generally, which means additional points of stress in any given situation.

The third column of course is the stress caused by the event when you have quit nicotine. As you can see it is lower than either the habitual nicotine user in withdrawal, or the user after a dose of nicotine. There is no withdrawal at all, and no lack of confidence and resilience caused by the erosion of your fitness and health generally, and no additional anxiety caused by the daily consumption of nicotine.

The problem with the subconscious is that it cannot differentiate and appreciate all these subtle ramifications. On one level it is an amazing system, but on another it is incredibly stupid. It goes purely on cause and immediate effect. It simply concludes that nicotine makes you feel better and therefore keeps triggering you to reach for the next dose. It is incapable of appreciating that the entire mechanism of nicotine addiction is to cause stress and anxiety which it then partially relieves.

There is a deeply held belief by both smokers and vapers that inhaling smoke or vape is inherently enjoyable. It becomes the third way of consuming something for pleasure; we eat, we drink, and we inhale smoke or vape. In the next chapter we are going to build on the concepts covered in this chapter to see if there is anything inherently enjoyable about breathing in nicotine. If your form of nicotine consumption does not involve inhaling the nicotine (for example if you use snus, dip, pouches, gum or patches) then you may be tempted to skip this chapter, but I would urge you not to as it will help to further your understanding of addiction generally.

10. Inhaling Smoke / Vapour

The only attraction to smoking or vaping is the nicotine and the only pleasure from smoking or vaping is the relieving of the withdrawal pangs from nicotine. Some people find this a difficult concept to grasp; that there is no pleasure in inhaling tobacco smoke or vapour aside from the nicotine element. As mentioned at the end of the last chapter they view smoking as almost a third way of nourishing themselves, a third way of consuming something that is enjoyable, along with eating and drinking. We eat, we drink, and we inhale smoke or vapour. To fully dissect and understand this aspect we firstly need to have a good working knowledge of our respiratory system.

Without wanting to start at too basic a level we have lungs. These are organs that we breath air into, the lungs absorb the oxygen from the air which is passed into our blood supply and pumped all around our body.

There are two ways for air to get into our lungs. The first is via our nose. The nose is fully equipped to deal with this. It has extremely sensitive sensors to detect exactly what we are breathing in. If what we are breathing has nothing but air in it then all well and good, if it has something nice in it (like the smell of nice food) then we can identify that and act upon it. If something smells unpleasant then this usually means it is poisonous or in some way bad for us, so again we can take steps to avoid it. In extreme examples what we breathe in is so poisonous that a more marked reaction is generated; our nose may sting, our eyes water, and we involuntarily shy away from it in an automated attempt to get away from it and it find a cleaner, purer air source.

The human nose isn't just equipped with sensors, it is also equipped with defence mechanisms designed to remove any impurities that there may be in the air. It has fine hairs on the inside of it and also generates mucus. The combination of these two traps any tiny particles that may be in the air so as to prevent them from entering your lungs.

This defence mechanism is where one of the problems with the nose as a source of air comes in. The tubes have to be fairly narrow so that any particles are effectively trapped (if the tubes were too wide a significant number of particles would just pass through them). The sinuses are also susceptible to infection (which is what the common cold is). When an infection takes hold the sinuses swell up as more blood is directed to that area so that the white blood cells in the blood can fight the infection. This causes our nose to become blocked. The nose also sticks out a bit and is therefore susceptible to injury, and injury can cause it to swell up and therefore become blocked (as anyone who has had a broken nose, or even a sharp crack on it, can testify). There are also times during intense physical activity that the amount of oxygen that we need to keep up with the activity in question exceeds the amount that can fit down the narrow passages of the nose. For all these reasons we have a secondary way of getting air into our lungs: through our mouths.

Breathing through your mouth allows a far greater amount of air to make it to your lungs, but it is without the defence mechanism and sensors of the nose (which is why people hold their nose when they smell something unpleasant; by breathing through their mouth they bypass their sense of smell and can't detect the foul smell).

This may seem like an odd system but in fact it works extremely well. Most of the time breathing through the nose is perfectly adequate; we get the oxygen we need and it is properly filtered. On the occasions that we need to we can take in far greater quantities via a different route. This alternative route through the mouth may not be able to filter out all the impurities but that's fine, the lungs can deal with those small amounts of particles and impurities with absolutely no detrimental impact at all. The lungs themselves have their own limited defence mechanisms that are designed to kick in on those occasions when we need to obtain oxygen by the secondary back up route through the mouth. It is the minority of the time that we need to mouth breath and the lungs are equipped to deal with this as long as it is for limited periods.

So now we have a basic understanding of how our respiratory system works; the nose is the primary method for taking in air, complete with sensor and filtering system. The mouth is the secondary back up system with neither sensor nor filtering system; what you breathe in through your mouth has no sensor to check for poison or other impurities, it just provides a direct, unfiltered route to the lungs. The lungs have their own limited defence mechanism which is designed to cope with the odd occasion of increased physical activity, or illness or injury, when inhalation through the nose becomes difficult.

So the real way to see if inhaling tobacco smoke is in any way natural is to sniff it up your nose. This runs it by the part of you that checks what you are breathing in to see if it is welcome or unwelcome, or to put it another way, to see if what you are breathing in is good for you or a poison. Let me be quite clear here, I am not just talking about sniffing air that has a small amount of tobacco smoke in it, that is not the true test, in this case the amount of smoke in the air is so diluted that it doesn't really bother the sensor that is in your nose. Your nose will identify it, but it won't trigger any sort of adverse reaction because the amount of it is too small to be a major problem. In the same way you can stand near a bonfire and smell the smoke, as long as you aren't being engulfed by it. The way to check whether cigarette smoke or vape is actually welcome by your body is to take a drag of cigarette smoke or inhale the vape directly up your nose.

If you've never done this then I wouldn't recommend it, it is intensely painful. It triggers the full physiological reaction to pure poison; intense sharp pain in the nose, eyes watering, and an involuntary shying away from the source of the smoke. Most smokers however won't even need to make the experiment, they will have encountered on numerous occasions the situation where some smoke drifts inadvertently straight up their nose, so will be familiar with the reaction.

Smoking and vaping is only physically possible by human beings because they have this secondary method of obtaining oxygen, it allows them to bypass a sensor that would otherwise make poisoning themselves impossible.

So breathing smoke or vape through our mouths makes smoking possible, but even then the act of breathing smoke or vapour in is not enjoyable. The only reason we smoke is because it is the most common way of obtaining nicotine. If you are in any doubt about this try smoking herbal cigarettes (those cigarettes with no nicotine) or nicotine free vape. They render the process entirely pointless because there is no nicotine.

I referred at the start of the book to my use of dip or snus. For those not familiar with this, it is a form of chewing tobacco but is very moist and very finely cut (some forms are almost like a powder). I once shared a flat with an American who introduced me to it. You take a little pinch of it and put it in your mouth, tucked in down the side of your gum, and the nicotine is absorbed through your skin. It is popular in both the US and Sweden. It causes mouth cancer and a Google search reveals some quite unpleasant pictures of people with gaping holes in their cheeks from 'dipping'.

Imagine something that you put in your mouth several times a day that slowly burns its way through your mouth, until you had a huge hole in your cheek. Can you imagine how much it would hurt each time you put it in your mouth? Why do people dip to the point of having holes in their face? Doesn't the pain stop them?

I can tell you from personal experience what happens. The first few times you take it doesn't hurt at all, you can feel the effects of the nicotine without any kind of pain or burning or stinging. But this doesn't last for very long at all, very soon it starts to sting and burn as the skin is regularly exposed to the dip.

However it is what is going on in your brain that is the key point. In the usual course of events a burning, stinging feeling in your mouth triggers the expected reaction, which is 'ouch, that isn't nice, I'm going to stop doing it'. But the problem is that this particular burning feeling is also accompanied with the nicotine entering your bloodstream which in turn ends the nicotine withdrawal. So your brain very quickly learns that the burning feeling in your mouth equates to ending the feeling of grogginess, woolly headedness, timidity and worry.

As we dealt with in the previous chapter, one of the driving elements of our survival as a species is our ability to adapt. Our planet has the potential to change hugely, meaning our diet, our environment, and our way of life could also change dramatically. A species may suddenly find that its main food supply that it has been reliant on for thousands of years suddenly disappears. To survive, we have to have an innate ability to adapt. Again let's think about it in relation to food. Let's say that you are an animal whose primary food since time immemorial has been apples. Suddenly there is an outbreak of a disease that kills all the apple trees. Your food is gone. You grow hungrier and hungrier. Of course hunger is another driving force in our survival, and one of the aspects of this is that increasing hunger causes desperation. The more hungry you are the more desperate you become and the more you will eat anything to stay alive. You eat some hemlock and become even more ill, you try some belladonna and also become ill. Then you try a carrot. It's covered in earth, it doesn't taste like much, but it doesn't make you sick and you feel better for eating it because it has some nutritional value. So you start eating carrots.

You may think this is a silly example because we know what we can and can't eat, but animals don't know this and neither did we as human beings until very recently (in evolutionary terms). The point is that we can learn to like anything that seems to confer a benefit.

However going back to taking dip, I can testify from personal experience that your brain stops interpreting that burning feeling as being unpleasant, and starts to interpret it as something good. It actually becomes quite a pleasant feeling, hard as it may be to believe. That stinging, burning feeling starts to feel piquant, tingly, warming. Your brain links that burn in your mouth to the relieving of the nicotine withdrawal. It doesn't factor in that it is the nicotine that has caused the withdrawal in the first place, the only interpretation it takes from this sequence of events is: mouth burn = huge benefit. Indeed if you think about it, it's not entirely different from 'acquiring' the taste for whiskey or other spirits. When you drink a neat spirit it burns and tastes vile, but we soon start to associate that burning feeling with the chemical effects of the alcohol, and so it becomes 'enjoyable'.

Smoking a cigarette or hitting a vape is exactly the same principle. There is nothing pleasant about breathing smoke or nicotine laden vapour into your lungs (and as I say if you are in any doubt about this try a nicotine free herbal cigarette or a nicotine free vape). The first time anyone inhales smoke or vape they invariably cough. This is a perfectly normal and natural reaction. We are genetically programmed to cough if we inadvertently inhale something poisonous. Coughing is an automated reaction that forcibly exhales whatever is in our lungs. This automated reaction is there as a survival mechanism; we need oxygen to survive and the only way of absorbing oxygen from the atmosphere is through our lungs. Quite simply if our lungs are damaged and cannot absorb oxygen we die, so we have this automated extreme reaction to forcibly remove anything from our lungs that can damage them.

When we first try a vape or cigarette even though we may cough, some of the nicotine will hit our lungs and be absorbed into our blood stream. We will feel slightly more alert and focussed. The brain will reinterpret what has happened in light of the overall effect: that the inhaling of this particular substance actually seemed to confer a benefit (by making us feel more focussed). So the next time you inhale any nicotine laden gas, your brain inhibits the coughing mechanism.

11. Addictiveness

We have covered in an earlier chapter the addictive nature of nicotine from a physiological perspective (that the brain seeks to counter the effect of the drug, to incorporate it, so that when the drug wears off it leaves a void that can only be filled by another dose). We have also now covered off how one of the main strands of addiction lies in our subconscious; as soon as our subconscious mind makes the link between the unpleasant feeling that starts to build up after we finish a dose of nicotine being relieved by another dose, every dose of nicotine causes the desire for the next as it wears off.

This gives us a basic understanding of our own nicotine consumption and addiction more generally, but there are two further concepts that we can cover which will not only help us develop our understanding of this basic principle, but will also help understand how severe (or otherwise) the physical withdrawal is. They will also help to explain why nicotine is so 'addictive' (and indeed what makes some drugs more 'addictive' than others). The first of these concepts is the 'Half-Life'. The second is the 'Method of Consumption'.

The Half-Life

The 'half-life' of a drug is the time it takes for the amount of the drug in your system to drop by a half. So you take a drug, it goes into your bloodstream where its effects are then felt, but it doesn't remain there forever. It is processed and eventually removed. The time it takes for the amount of the drug in your system to drop by half is the drug's half-life. In essence, the half-life is how quickly it takes for a drug to wear off (the shorter the half-life, the quicker it wears off). Nicotine has a comparatively short half-life when compared to other drugs that you are likely to come into contact with and consume. To give some examples:

Drug	Half-Life
Nicotine	2 Hours
Alcohol	5 hours
Caffeine	5 hours

So what is the relevance of a short half-life? A short half-life is both good news and bad news from an addiction perspective. Let's deal with the bad news first.

Generally speaking, the shorter the half-life the more addictive the drug. Remember what we covered off about the role of the subconscious; that it works by cause and effect. The cause is when we consume the drug, the effect is when it hits our blood stream. Remember also that once the subconscious makes the link between the unpleasant feeling that slowly builds up after one dose of a drug wears off being relieved by the next dose, the 'addiction' takes hold. By this I mean that the wearing off of one dose causes the desire for the next.

With this in mind you can see how a drug that causes an immediate hit, then a pronounced low, followed by another pronounced hit when we take the next dose, is going to be far more addictive (from a subconscious mind perspective) than a drug where the highs and lows are far more gentle, subtle, and more spread out over time. This is because it is less noticeable and so will take longer for your subconscious mind to make the connection.

So this is the bad news when a drug has a short half-life – it makes it far easier to get addicted to it.

On the other side, the good news of nicotine having a short half-life is that the withdrawal is less severe. A strong cigarette has about 20mg of nicotine in it but in fact a smoker will only absorb about 1mg of nicotine from that cigarette (some burns away without being inhaled, and what is inhaled is mostly exhaled without being absorbed). The strongest nicotine pouches also contain about 20mg of nicotine, but the consumer only absorbs about 30% of this (so about 7 mg). It is also worth bearing in mind that it is estimated that a dose of nicotine of about 50-60mg would be fatal.

Let's assume that you have a very high consumption of nicotine and that you have 20mg of nicotine in your body. This means that after 2 hours you have 10 mg of nicotine in your body. After 4 hours you have 5mg. After 6 hours 2.5mg. After 8 hours (the time most people are in bed for) you have 1.25mg. And if you start with 2mg of nicotine (which is more likely) then after 8 hours you would have 0.125mg of nicotine in you (which is a negligible amount).

The point here is that even the very heaviest consumers of nicotine will wake up in the morning with virtually no nicotine in their system which means that their body and brain is regularly used to having no nicotine in their system.

Let's now compare that to caffeine. A standard cup of coffee has around 100mg of caffeine in it, and unlike nicotine, 100% of that will be absorbed. If you have three cups of coffee, that gives you 300mg of caffeine. In 5 hours that will be 150mg. In 10 hours it will be 75mg. So even if you cut off your caffeine consumption at 2pm, at 10 pm at night you still have 75mg of caffeine in your system. At 3am you have 37.5mg. In short, for the average caffeine drinker, the level of caffeine in their system remains at significant amount throughout their lives, even when it is at its lowest (usually when they wake up having not consumed caffeine during their sleeping hours). If you have consumed caffeine for years or even decades, your body will literally have had it in its system in significant quantities for this entre period, and if you are deprived of caffeine the withdrawal is severe because your body is simply not used to being without it. This is not the case with nicotine, because for even the heaviest consumer of nicotine, the levels of nicotine within the body drop to negligible amounts on a daily basis.

You may be questioning this because if you can't have your morning dose of nicotine you suffer far more than if you miss your morning cup of coffee. There are two reasons for this. Firstly, because the caffeine remains in your system for that much longer, it takes much longer for the full withdrawal to kick in. It usually takes around 24 hours without caffeine for the full effects of the withdrawal to kick in (which is something very few regular consumers of caffeine will ever do). Secondly remember the physiological effects of anticipation. If you are about to take your first dose of nicotine of the day and for some reason have to skip it, you will suffer far more because of the expectation of the immediate nicotine hit.

The Method of Consumption

As I've mentioned previously the effect of a drug is felt when it hits your bloodstream. The amount of time between the act of consuming a drug and it hitting your bloodstream is critical when it comes to assessing its 'addictiveness'. Remember that a significant part of addiction is when your subconscious makes the link between the unpleasant feeling that starts to build up when one dose of the drug starts to wear off being relieved by the next dose. When this learning process is complete every dose of the drug causes the desire for the next dose. If the act of consuming the drug is very quickly followed by your feeling the effect, the addiction (or the subconscious aspect of it at least) will take effect much quicker because the subconscious works by cause and effect; the more obvious the cause and effect the quicker it will notice it and learn from it.

There are five main methods of consuming a drug; injecting, snorting, inhaling, absorbing, and eating / drinking. In chronological order in terms of how long it takes for the effect to be felt, these methods of consumption are as follows:

Injecting: This places the drug directly into the bloodstream so the effect is felt almost immediately.

Inhaling: The smoke or vapour is taken into the lungs where it is absorbed into the bloodstream in the same way that oxygen is. The effect is felt within seconds of inhaling.

Snorting: The drug is absorbed into the bloodstream via the sinuses, again the effect is virtually immediate.

Absorbing: This applies to things like nicotine patches and pouches. The drug is placed on the skin or in the mouth, where it is absorbed through the skin into the bloodstream. Again the effect is felt within a few seconds.

Eating / drinking: This applies primarily to alcohol and caffeine, and medication consumed orally. The drug has to make its way into the stomach where a small proportion of the drug is absorbed, with the rest being absorbed when the drug makes its way to the small intestine. How long this takes is dependent on various factors, for example how full your stomach is, but on average is takes 15-20 minutes for the drug to be absorbed. You may be reading this thinking that this cannot be right, that when you have an alcoholic drink or a cup of coffee you feel the effect much sooner. You may well be feeling the initial effect, but the drug will not be fully absorbed for some time.

Can you see how there is this large disparity in our experience of drugs and how addictive they are, simply on the basis of the method of consumption and the half-life? If you inject or inhale something with a short half-life, you have this large, noticeable effect, followed by a pronounced dip as it wears off. Another dose gives you another pronounced and obvious lift by relieving the withdrawal. This effect is noticeable and obvious to your subconscious so it makes the connection far quicker, and consequently the addiction takes hold much sooner

Compare this to drinking a drug with a long half-life. The effect slowly builds up for 15 to 20 minutes after you have drunk it, so there is a much larger disparity between consuming the drug and the full effect of it being felt. It then slowly wears off over quite an extended period of time. In this way it takes much longer for the subconscious to make the link between taking the drug and relieving the withdrawal.

The impact of the immediate hit and how it can make a substance more or less 'addictive' can be seen very clearly when we look at the history of vaping. Dr Robert Jackler (a Stanford

Professor who has studied e-cigarettes and nicotine) explained it this way:

> "Earlier generations of so-called electronic cigarettes used what's called freebase nicotine which was difficult to inhale. It had a bite in your throat. And what it did is it inhibited the ability to raise the nicotine level up because it got too bitter.
>
> What they found is if you conjugate nicotine with a weak organic acid, so called salt nicotine, that it tasted much softer. It burned the throat less. That overcame that harshness of the traditional e-cigarette. It's a kind of a chemical trickery that allows the body's normal defence mechanisms to be overcome, and it is very smooth and goes down very easily."

He then goes on to say:

> "Original vapes were popular with teenagers and high school kids but they weren't getting addicted in the same way. With the advent of Juul [the first company to develop the use of nicotine salt in order to substantially increase the amount of nicotine that could be delivered through a vape] the younger vapers were becoming very addicted very quickly."

Now we have covered two important elements of 'addictiveness'; the half-life and the method of consumption. Society generally considers that alcohol and caffeine are not addictive in the normal sense of the word, but from a chemical perspective they absolutely are in that they cause a pronounced withdrawal which another dose of the drug will relieve. However their long half-life and the fact that we drink them as opposed to inhale or inject them, blurs the lines between 'enjoyment' and 'addiction'. With nicotine this is not the case. The short half-life and the fact that we consume it using one of the much quicker ways of getting it into our bloodstream, means we find ourselves 'addicted' to it (in the more generally accepted sense of the word) far quicker.

Having said this, it is not all bad news from a nicotine perspective, because the short half-life means that the physical withdrawal is far more manageable, because we regularly have negligible amounts of the drug in our system.

You may well be reading this wondering what on earth I am talking about. When I say that 'the physical withdrawal is far more manageable' this may be completely at odds with your own experience, and the view of society generally, which is that giving up nicotine is incredibly difficult. The key word here is 'physical'. I am talking here only about the physical withdrawal, not the 'craving' (that conscious thought process whereby we fantasise, tease, and obsess), nor 'the physiological effects of anticipation'.

One of the problems with quitting nicotine isn't just the first few days when our brain is adjusting to not having nicotine anymore, but in the long term we can often feel that something is missing from our lives. Nicotine consumers who quit for months or even years are often still vulnerable to being dragged back. There are actually some specific psychological reasons for this that you need to be aware of so you can be sure of successfully quitting not only in the short term, but the long term as well. We will cover these off in the next chapter.

12. Fading Affect Bias and Ambition

Fading Affect Bias describes a process by which our view of the past becomes increasingly positive as time passes. We remember situations from the past far more positively than we actually experienced them. It is the psychological embodiment of nostalgia, or 'the good old days'. Why it exists is unclear, one prevailing theory suggests that it allows people to maintain a positive outlook on life; by seeing past events (and our role in them) in a more positive light, we are able to maintain a more positive outlook on life more generally. Why it exists is probably less important for the purpose of unravelling the nicotine phenomenon than the fact of its existence. All we really need to appreciate is that past events in our lives are always remembered more positively than they actually were at the time.

Whilst this may be a positive thing in most aspects of our lives as it allows us to maintain a more positive outlook generally, with drugs generally and nicotine in particular, it can cause problems. As soon as we quit time starts to pass, and we then start to think back on nicotine with fondness and nostalgia. The memory of the lethargy, the tight chest, the coughing, the feeling of being in the grip of something we don't fully understand, starts to fade. We forget the bad and all that is left is the good.

This is particularly relevant to nicotine if you consider how many doses of nicotine you take that you actually enjoy. Nicotine is at its most crucial when the withdrawal is at its highest point, this means that the longer you go without it the more you 'enjoy' it. The problem is that the withdrawal starts as soon as you finish consuming the dose of nicotine and continues to increase over time. So the withdrawal and subconscious triggers can kick off almost as soon as you finish a dose. Whether the craving process also kicks in will depend on various factors, the most obvious being whether you are able to take nicotine freely or not. So if you smoke cigarettes or vape and are at work and have to go outside to smoke or vape then you won't be able to just spend all day outside smoking / vaping. There will be an interval of time before you can have each dose. In this case you may be fine for some time before the withdrawal / subconscious triggers / passage of time is such that you feel that it is 'time' for your next dose, and when that time arrives, when you get to the mindset that you are about due your next cigarette, that thought will start to occupy your mind and so the craving will start. This is often why we can end up going for some quite extended periods at work not taking nicotine; if you are busy and your mind is fully taken up with the job in hand, you will be concentrating on what needs doing and so won't have the mental bandwidth to also start the craving process. You won't be craving nicotine because you have no mental capacity spare to start thinking about how lovely it would be to take that next dose.

The problem is that when there are no restrictions on your nicotine intake, when the packet or vape is in front of you and you can reach for it any time you like, when everyone around you is smoking or vaping, or if you use dip or pouches, there is no restriction on your intake and so there is a natural tendency to consume nicotine almost constantly. If you smoke, as soon as one cigarette is put out and the nicotine starts to leave your body, the subconscious triggers start. As you have no reason not to smoke you will find that you are almost immediately thinking about whether to smoke or not. This makes a distressing mental conundrum which is distracting you from what should otherwise be a period of enjoyment, and the easiest way to end this is to just take another cigarette. In this way for the vast majority of cigarettes that you smoke, you are hardly even aware of smoking them. This is true for all methods of consuming nicotine, not just smoking. When you are taking doses of nicotine regularly and often you are not relieving a severe withdrawal and so there is no particular pleasure in it. These doses of nicotine that we take but get no particular pleasure in are what I call 'maintenance doses'.

You may now think that I've just provided you with the ideal solution; cut out the maintenance doses, that way you will enjoy every dose and will have cut back hugely on the health risk and costs. Unfortunately this solution doesn't work because even though these doses give you no particular pleasure, they are still necessary for you to enjoy yourself, concentrate on work, etc because without them you will be craving, obsessing, miserable, and unable to properly engage in what you are supposed to be doing. These doses may be devoid of any enjoyment, but they are as necessary as the supposedly enjoyable ones. They are even more negative than other doses because they give you no particular pleasure or boost, but without them you are miserable and unable to function properly.

Let me be absolutely clear on one point, when I refer to nicotine as 'enjoyable' remember that the enjoyment is rebalancing an internal chemical imbalance caused by your previous dose (in other words relieving the withdrawal). Even these 'enjoyable' doses leave you no better off than if you weren't chemically dependent on nicotine, and it is a pleasure that you will experience all the time when you quit.

Be that as it may, for most regular consumers of nicotine the vast majority of doses that they take in a day aren't the really crucial, enjoyable, withdrawal-relieving doses like the first one of the day.

The vast majority of them are the 'maintenance' ones, the ones that we aren't even aware that we are taking, or the ones that make us feel actively disgusted and sick of the whole business because we know that we are consuming far more than we should.

But when you try to quit nicotine, which doses do you find yourself thinking about all the time? It's not the maintenance doses, it's the really crucial enjoyable ones. Indeed when we stop, the maintenance doses are virtually forgotten and the only ones we remember are those that we really wanted, that we really needed, when the withdrawal and craving was at its worst. It is these idyllic doses, the first cigarette or vape we had in the morning, or the one we had on the balcony on holiday with an ice-cold drink next to us, that we remember. This is how FAB works; it causes us to remember and focus on all the best parts of a past situation and forget the mediocre or bad parts.

You need to be aware of this phenomenon because when you quit and start thinking back on your life as a nicotine addict you need to keep firmly in mind the reality and not the FAB induced fantasy. Remember the heavy feeling, that the vast majority of doses were no more than maintenance doses, remember the wasted money and the wanting to quit, the lack of fitness and the feeling of having to have something that in your heart of hearts you really want to be free of.

In fact there is another driving factor that exacerbates this; ambition. When I am talking about ambition I am not talking about it in its narrow, job related sense of wanting to take the next step on whatever particular career ladder we've chosen (or fallen into). I am using the term in a far more general sense; as a basic driving force within all living things to try to improve their lot in life.

The species that are driven to improve their lives, and the lives of their families, are the species that are most likely to survive and thrive. If you are a hunter gatherer, living on stony soil with very little to hunt or gather, and you see a few miles distant a green and fertile land, you have to have that driving force to move to that other land; to travel, to fight, to face the unknown and to take it for your own. This desire to improve our lives, to strive for something better, to constantly be looking for ways to improve things, is a survival force as basic as hunger, thirst, and the sex drive.

Ambition isn't just about wanting something better, it is far more intricate than that. It is made up of two separate tendencies; the tendency to look for fault in what we already have, and to glorify and idealise what we don't have. It is these two tendencies together that make up the phenomenon that we think of as 'ambition'. It is a normal, natural motivating force for all living creatures, and promotes improvement for the individual, the family, and the species. These two factors make sure we find fault in what we have, and are constantly driven to obtain the next thing. This is the very definition of ambition.

In fact this phenomenon can be seen in all aspects of human life. How many times have you wanted that perfect job, got it, been ecstatic, then been looking for the next job within a year or two? Or moved heaven and earth to move to a new house, and then eventually found yourself just as unhappy with the new place as you were with the old? How many times have you fought to get that one true love, then found you can't get away from them quick enough? And then found when you do split up from them, that you want them back? Or on the other end, how many times have you chased after someone again and again only to be rejected, then given up on them and left them alone, only for them to then show an interest? They don't want you while you're available, and only when you become unavailable do they suddenly want you. Ever looked at a billionaire and wondered why they were still working and trying to make even more money? They are as susceptible to this tendency as any of us. We all want to improve and strive for more.

'Familiarity breeds contempt', 'the temptation of the forbidden fruit', 'the end of the honeymoon period'. All these common phrases essentially describe the same process; that natural tendency to pick holes in what we do have and glorify what we don't have. This is the key concept. If something falls into the 'I have it' category then we view it harshly, we criticise it, and look to find fault with it. If something falls into the 'I don't have it' category then we glorify it, idolise it, and desire it.

This is a natural and healthy tendency. It drives us to improve. The problem is the way in which this tendency interacts with drugs and contributes to addiction. Let's now apply this driving force to nicotine.

While we're regularly taking nicotine it falls into the 'I have it' category. We tend towards finding fault with it and, frankly, that is all too easy to do. The shortness of breath, the exhaustion, the impact on our health, the smell, the heavy, drained feeling, the financial cost, and all for the dubious 'pleasure' of returning for a few moments to the feeling of peace and confidence that we'd experience all the time if only we could quit. Well there's an obvious solution to that problem, the solution is staring us in the face: quit! So we quit. But the problem is that having quit, nicotine has now moved from the 'I have it' category, into the 'I don't have it' category. Consequently we stop thinking of it critically and we start idolising it. The lethargy, the financial cost, the shortness of breath, the tight feeling in our lungs, the smell, that fact that the vast majority of the doses we took were maintenance doses and gave us no particular pleasure anyway, and all the other downsides of our nicotine consumption are suddenly forgotten. Now we are thinking only of those doses that we really enjoyed; the first one of the day, the one on the balcony on holiday, the one after a busy day at work when we'd been so busy we went far longer than we usually would without our dose of nicotine. If you pause for a minute you'll realise how irrational this thinking is and how badly the truth has been warped by this phenomenon of 'ambition' and FAB. How many doses of nicotine have you taken over the course of your life? How many fall into the 'really enjoyable' category as opposed to the 'maintenance category'? I appreciate that the line between the two isn't always that clear, and these days with the places where you can freely smoke or vape becoming increasingly restricted, probably more and more doses fall into the 'enjoyable' category. Even so, isn't it the case that only a very small minority of them fall into the truly 'enjoyable' category?

This basic driving force means we forget the bad. Instead of looking at the reality we idolise, we fantasise, we select from our memory those very few occasions where we really 'enjoyed' that dose of nicotine. We ignore the fact that the enjoyment was really just momentarily correcting a chemical imbalance caused by all the previous doses of nicotine and we forget that the vast majority of doses weren't even enjoyable and may even have been actively repulsive. We focus in on that tiny 2% or 3% of the overall experience that we thought was actually enjoyable. We want something we won't let ourselves have, something we now view as highly desirable, so we become miserable. This thinking starts the craving process and our lives go on hold while we sit there in self-imposed misery. We think that all of this misery is because we stopped taking nicotine. We see a simple solution to this misery, a remedy, and that is to start consuming nicotine again.

The problem is that when we start again, we return to the reality of nicotine, not the idolised fantasy. What we return to is not the paradise we've been pining for, but the living hell we wanted to escape from in the first place. The fantasy evaporates and reality comes crashing back in. Our nicotine addiction moves from the 'I don't have it' into the 'I have it' category. This may not happen immediately, after all that first dose will remove any withdrawal (or it may not if you have stopped for long enough for the withdrawal to wear off anyway) and it will also remove the mental craving and the constant internal mental indecision about whether to take a dose or not. So all in all we probably will feel far better for taking that first dose, but the vast majority (if not all) of the pleasure in taking that dose will be to end a purely mental process that could have been ended, or even prevented from starting in the first place, by ways other than taking more nicotine. Be that as it may, very soon you will return to the reality of nicotine, not the idolised fantasy you were dreaming about. It may happen while taking that first dose, or it may take a few hours, or even a few days, but it will happen. Pretty soon you are back to where you started, which is doing something you hate and desperately looking for a way to quit. And so the process continues.

This is the central frustration of the addict, whether their drug is nicotine, alcohol, heroin or methamphetamine. What they miss and keep returning to never existed to begin with. It is pure fantasy that exists only in their mind. It is essentially the shift in perception between how we see something that we have, and how we see something that we are denying ourselves. Just remember this one thing if nothing else: if nicotine addiction was as good as you remember it being after you've stopped, you'd never have stopped in the first place.

13. Nicotine and Obesity

Let's now turn our minds to how nicotine affects our weight and body shape. To do this we need to go back to the basic drug types, stimulants and depressants, and consider in a bit more detail how these affect hunger and appetite.

As we've dealt with previously, stimulants are drugs that wake us up, increase our alertness, increase our heart rate, and in stronger doses leave us feeling anxious, afraid, and confused. When we are under stress or pressure our fight or flight response is triggered, the point being that whatever is confronting us that we fear we will either need to fight it or run away from it, so the stimulants our brain releases assist with this response. Our heart rate increases in readiness for the imminent escalation in activity, our alertness surges, our perception of time even slows down so everything seems to happen in slow motion. One of the main lessons taught in public speaking classes is to speak slowly, because when the adrenaline kicks in our perception of time alters, we speak faster in real time, but our perception is that we are speaking at a normal pace. In cases of more extreme fear, we can also involuntarily void our bowels or urinate. This is the body not only ridding itself of excess weight, but more importantly removing the need to expend energy on any bodily function (like digestion) other than the anticipated physical activity.

In addition to this, stimulants also remove our appetite. This is fairly obvious when you think about it, when coming face to face with a man-eating tiger the last thing you need is to be overcome by an urge to sit down to a large meal. There is in fact another aspect to this; digestion takes a huge amount of energy (hence why we feel sleepy and tired after a large meal). When you eat something it has to travel through approximately 20 foot of digestive tract, and muscles in the digestive system work hard to force it every inch of the way. Digestion takes up large amounts of energy so when physical activity is imminent (which your body assumes there will be when you are scared or stressed) your appetite decreases. The brain usually waits for a period of relaxation before triggering the hunger mechanism. Your brain knows that you need a period of rest after eating so that blood, energy and bodily resources can be directed to digestion. In this way exercise and stress will remove your appetite and rest and relaxation will trigger it. This is why you can be busy at work all day without even thinking about food then realise you are ravenously hungry as soon as you go home and start to relax.

This of course leads us on to depressants. These are the groups of drugs that inhibit or depress nerve activity. They make us feel relaxed, sleepy, and unafraid, and in stronger dosses can leave us intoxicated or uncoordinated. They also make us hungry because times of rest and relaxation are the best times for us to eat. This of course isn't true for very powerful depressants which can depress our nerve activity to such an extent that we no longer feel hunger, but it is true of alcohol which is a chemical depressant and causes people to demonstrate a marked increase in appetite. This explains the apparent anomaly which is that alcohol is a sedative, but is often referred to as an 'appetite stimulant'.

So stimulants tend to decrease our appetite, and depressants tend to increase it. That being the case you'd expect that nicotine would help you lose weight because as we have covered previously nicotine is a stimulant. Unfortunately it rarely works this way for several reasons.

Firstly of course and as covered right at the start of this book, the brain does not just passively accept regular doses of nicotine without reacting in any way. It takes steps to counter this regular injection of an outside stimulant with the result that, in a very short space of time, the nicotine makes you feel normal, and you feel groggy and disorientated and out of sorts without it. So in fact your appetite very soon goes back to normal. At least, it goes back to normal when you are consuming nicotine, but it increases as the nicotine wears off and your brain is then understimulated because at this point you are in a state of sedation due to the nicotine having worn off. So in fact as a regular consumer of nicotine you very quickly end up at the stage where your hunger is normal when you have nicotine in your system, but your hunger is artificially increased when you do not.

A lot of people believe that nicotine curbs their appetite, but this is usually based on their experience of stopping for short periods. When you quit nicotine you have a few days physical withdrawal to pass through before you get back to normal. This is the period of readjustment where the brain recognises that the additional false stimulation provided by the nicotine is no longer in play, so it slowly gets back to releasing its own stimulants until you eventually end up with that feeling of confidence, resilience and buoyancy that you had before you started taking nicotine, and that, since you became addicted to nicotine, you have only experienced partially whilst taking a dose of nicotine. When you are going through this withdrawal period you will have a lack of stimulants in your system, so you will find your hunger is correspondingly increased. This is why so many people believe that nicotine helps them lose weight or curbs their eating. When they don't take nicotine they are hungry due to the lack of stimulants, and when they take some they get back to normal which means their appetite decreases. So they end up thinking that nicotine helps them lose weight. In fact it is only during this brief withdrawal period that there is any increase in appetite, this soon returns to normal, and in fact is entirely dwarfed by the increased ability to exercise which I will cover off next.

The second point is that nicotine makes you feel heavy and lethargic and robs you of energy, and thus makes exercise far harder and far more unpleasant. It does this by increasing your heart rate and blood pressure.

Say your resting heart rate is 60 (your resting heart rate is how many times your heart pumps in one minute while you are resting, with lower readings being an indicator of fitness and good health, and higher readings being an indicator or poor health and unfitness). One dose of nicotine, if you have not had any for some time, will usually push your heart rate up to somewhere near to double what it should be. It also, as mentioned previously, causes a significant spike in blood pressure.

As we've touched on before, when your heart rate and blood pressure are high you want to sit down and rest. In this way, consumers of nicotine become constantly tired, lacking in energy and lethargic. You do hear about people having cigarettes or vaping and going for a run or going to the gym, but they tend to be younger, fitter, and have been taking nicotine for far less time. Even with these unusual individuals they will be finding any exercise they do far harder, they will be working out at a far lower level, be making far less progress, and will be eroding their fitness at a far greater pace than if they didn't have nicotine in their bloodstream.

The fact is that nicotine either stops you exercising, or at the very least makes exercise harder, less effective and undoes any work you might be putting in by actively eroding your fitness. It artificially increases your heart rate and blood pressure and leaves you feeling lazy and lethargic when you would otherwise feel energetic and healthy. This chemical induced laziness is a huge cause of obesity because when you aren't exercising you don't need to eat much in order to start putting on weight. Nicotine addicts often view people who exercise regularly as some kind of weird obsessives, people who undergo huge amounts of pain and discomfort for reasons of vanity or in a desperate attempt to live a little bit longer. They really can't understand what motivates them. But this is only because exercise, for the nicotine addict, is deeply difficult due to their greatly elevated heart rate and blood pressure. It is considerably uncomfortable and even painful. But for anyone who doesn't have their heart rate and blood pressure substantially increased by a drug ,exercise is not painful or difficult, it is actually enjoyable and liberating. People exercise not because they want to lose weight or live longer but because, without a poisonous drug dragging you down, exercise is truly enjoyable. When you exercise your brain releases 'feel good' chemicals, like serotonin, dopamine, and adrenaline to make you feel alive, awake, confident and capable. People who exercise regularly do so for one reason and one reason alone; because it makes them feel great. There is a huge correlation between exercise and fitness, and self-confidence and good mental health.

The last aspect of this element to bear in mind is that one dose of nicotine will elevate your heart rate above its norm for approximately 36 hours, so you cannot escape this element by cutting down your intake. Even one dose a day, or even one every two days, will have a detrimental effect.

The final point to make in this chapter on nicotine and weight is that when we speak about losing weight what most people are talking about is losing fat. Most people want to lose fat but keep or even gain some muscle. This produces the lean, muscular physique that most people aim for. Not many people want to drop both fat and muscle because then they end up looking stick thin and skeletal. Generally speaking you lose fat by burning off more calories than you consume, so if you eat little enough you can still lose fat even without doing any exercise. It's hard but it can be done because even if you are motionless your body still burns energy performing bodily functions like breathing etc. So you can lose fat without exercising, but it is impossible to gain muscle without exercising. Even with steroids you have to exercise to build the muscle, so while smokers can smoke and lose weight, they often find it difficult to gain muscle because the increased heart rate caused by nicotine makes exercise difficult and far more unpleasant than it would otherwise be.

To sum up, nicotine makes you more likely to be overweight, more unfit, and to have less muscle. This may or may not have a negative impact on how you feel about your appearance, but it will definitely have an impact on how confident and happy you feel. As covered previously a positive and resilient mental outlook is tied inextricably with our physical state. Living things that are of ill health have an innate desire to hide away and rest. Animals who are fit and healthy have an innate desire to go out into the world, to explore, to eat, to procreate, to LIVE. In this way nicotine has a direct long-term detrimental impact on our mood and quality of life generally.

The other benefit to exercise is that it helps us to sleep better. The reduction in ability to exercise when consuming nicotine is not the only negative impact on sleep that nicotine has. We will cover off nicotine's impact on sleep in detail in the next chapter.

14. Nicotine and Sleep

Sleep is a hugely important aspect of our lives. Lack of sleep has been linked with cancer, depression, diabetes, obesity, and a myriad of other short and long-term problems. This is really just common sense. When we sleep, and most importantly when we get the right quality and quantity of sleep, our body repairs itself and our mind refreshes itself, with the result that we wake up feeling one of the greatest feelings it is possible to feel: refreshed, alert, and ready to face the day. If you are not getting the right amount or the right quality of sleep, you will quickly degenerate both physically and mentally. I emphasise here that it is not just quantity, but quality of sleep that is crucial. Most people assume that we go to bed, we lose consciousness for a few hours, then we come to and we're good to go. This is not the case at all and it is essential that you go through the right sleep cycles and the right stages of sleep.

Before we tackle the subject of how smoking and nicotine affects our sleep, we firstly need to get a good basic understanding of sleep. This isn't easy because, as with the topic of the human brain and the chemicals it produces and excretes, human understanding of sleep is in its infancy. There is much we as human beings do not understand about sleep but fortunately for our purposes a grasp of the basics will suffice.

One thing we do know about sleep is that we sleep in cycles which take us through different stages of sleep. One of the main differentiating factors between these sleep stages is how deeply we are asleep. So for example there is, as you would expect, 'deep sleep' which is the very deep sleep categorised by hugely reduced bodily functions. Another of the stages of sleep is REM (Rapid Eye Movement) sleep. REM sleep is categorised by rapid movement of the eyes, increased heart rate, and parts of the brain show activity that is similar to being awake. It is closely associated with dreaming. Essentially it is a period of sleep in which you are raised up from deep sleep into a state that is very close to being awake. No one actually knows what the purpose of REM sleep is, but what we do know is that is essential. In tests, rats that have been deprived of REM sleep die within 4 to 6 weeks. It is closely associated with good mental health. Lack of REM sleep causes depression, confusion and anxiety.

The basic fact that we need to have clear in our mind when considering the impact of nicotine on sleep is that unconsciousness doesn't equal good quality sleep, good quality sleep involves cycling up and down through various stages of unconsciousness while the body and brain recovers, repairs and recuperates. It helps sometimes to think of it like an aeroplane, gliding along up through the different layers of atmosphere, and back down again, having to go to each layer in a certain order, for a certain time, before gliding gently into the next one.

Nicotine affects sleep because nicotine is a stimulant, and it remains in our system after we consume our last dose. When you go to bed you will still have some nicotine coursing through your veins. Because it's a stimulant it keeps you awake. Even if you are a long-term heavy consumer of nicotine, well used to the effects of nicotine, the nicotine you have inside you from all the accumulated doses you have taken that day will make the act of dropping off to sleep difficult. This is why tests show that regular consumers of nicotine find it far more difficult to drop off to sleep than non-consumers do. Not only does nicotine make it harder to go to sleep, but more importantly at the start of the night the stimulating effects of the nicotine makes it far harder to cycle down into the deeper stages of sleep.

As the night wears on and the withdrawal kicks in, nicotine consumers are able to get into deeper and deeper sleep, but the problem here is that they are then understimulated, so they then find it difficult to go through the higher stages of sleep like REM sleep. This is why in tests smokers show significantly less time spent in the crucial REM sleep stage than non-smokers.

This covers off the chemical effects of nicotine on sleep, but there is another way in which smoking and vaping can affect our sleep. When you sleep the muscles and soft tissues in the throat relax and in some people they can collapse sufficiently to cause a total or partial blockage of the airway. When this happens the lack of oxygen triggers your brain to pull you out of deep sleep, either to a lighter sleep or to full wakefulness so your airway can reopen and you can breathe normally. This condition is known as apnoea. This repeated disturbance to your sleep can have a huge impact on your quality of sleep, leaving you very tired during the day, but because you may well be asleep all night (albeit unable to drop into deep sleep) you may have no idea that it is a problem.

Cigarette smoke and nicotine laden vapour irritates the lining of the nasal cavity and throat causing swelling and excess mucus. When the nasal passages become congested it is difficult to breathe through your nose because the airflow is decreased. This can disturb your sleep on its own, but it will also make you far more prone to apnoea.

The point to take away from this chapter is that sleep is crucial. Humans have evolved over millions of years and the human brain is one of the most complicated and intricate organisms on the planet. The human body and brain is revitalised and repaired during sleep, and sleep is an incredibly complex process. Nicotine interrupts and disrupts this process.

15. Cutting Down

We've previously touched on the concept of the 'enjoyable' doses and the 'maintenance' ones. We've also touched on the fact that nicotine not only appears enjoyable to the consumer, but also essential for them to cope with, and to enjoy, life. It is understandable therefore that the first choice of most nicotine addicts is not to stop entirely, but to cut down to just those enjoyable doses. This is a stage every addict passes through whatever their addiction. They start doing something out of curiosity, then because of enjoyment, but then they very soon reach the stage that it is not only enjoyable, but crucial, so they cannot do without it even when the truly destructive nature of it becomes apparent. They may want to stop, but they also cannot imagine a life without their little crutch. It is also the case that, because of the way the brain works (it compensates for either the depressive or stimulating effects of the drug) that we need more and more of the drug to get the same effect. This is essentially what tolerance is.

Most addicts get to the phase where they start to realise that their drug of choice is causing them serious problems, but of course they still 'enjoy' taking the drug and think it is an essential part of their lives. However they also recognise on either a conscious or subconscious level that the vast majority of the doses they take of their drug are maintenance doses, in other words they are not particularly enjoyable in comparison with other doses. The logical conclusion therefore is to cut down, to cut out the maintenance doses and just take the really enjoyable ones. This seems logical on the face of it, as smaller doses would seem to cut back on the negative aspects, but if you understand fully how the mechanism of addiction works you realise that it is doomed to failure.

This is why the cycle of all addiction isn't:

1. Take drug.
2. Become addicted.
3. Try to quit.

It is:

1. Take drug.
2. Become addicted.
3. Attempt and fail to moderate.
4. Try to quit.

The 'attempt and fail to moderate stage' can take years and many failed attempts to quit are in fact a simple regression from 'try to quit' back to 'attempt to moderate'. Often, when making the decision to abandon an attempt to quit, the mindset is that cutting down is actually sustainable long term; so the return to nicotine is on the basis that there is a method of cutting down that can actually work. To quit nicotine (or indeed any form of drug addiction) it is essential to firstly understand and fully appreciate why cutting down cannot work, and why it is never sustainable long term. The concept of 'cutting down' is a bar to quitting and we have to dispel it before we can move on to the only viable solution; to quit. There are several reasons why cutting down doesn't work:

Firstly, as we covered right at the start of the book, physical addiction comes about when your brain seeks to compensate for the effects of the drug, so that when the drug wears off you feel under par and out of sorts. Another dose of the drug then returns you to normal (which for most people is feeling fairly bright, confident and positive). In this way we see the drug as essential to enjoy life, and the numerous downsides fade into insignificance. The brain becomes increasingly proficient at countering the effects of the drug, so you need to steadily increase the dose to obtain the same effect. In this way even maintaining the current dose of any drug, let alone cutting down, becomes an increasingly difficult battle. The natural tendency is always to increase, not decrease, the dose.

Secondly a big part of addiction is when the subconscious makes the link between the unpleasant feeling that starts to kick in when one dose wears off, to having another dose to relieve that unpleasant feeling. When this happens the wearing off of every dose causes the desire for the next. This is learned behaviour and cannot be unlearned. The 'take it or leave it' stage you went through when you started taking nicotine is a once only experience, it can never be repeated.

One of the reasons people struggle with this is that they think of their nicotine consumption as habit. They think that they just got into the habit of taking, say, 20 doses a day. If they can just get into the habit of having 3 doses a day then this is what they will eventually be happy with and will only want or need 3 doses a day. Nicotine consumption is not habit but drug addiction. Do you think you could ever get into the habit of only eating 500 calories a week? Of course you couldn't. Why? Because there are physiological processes at play that mean you would want far, far more than that.

The same is true of nicotine addiction. If every time you finish a dose, the withdrawal is interpreted by the brain into a feeling of 'I need the next dose', that will not change. You can get rid of the feeling entirely by cutting out nicotine totally and waiting for your brain chemistry to get back to normal, but you can never make your brain 'unlearn' that another dose will get rid of the unpleasant feeling that builds up when the last dose finishes. The reason that you can never unlearn this is that it is absolutely true; the next dose WILL relieve the withdrawal caused by the previous one.

For the third point we need to return to the concept of craving. Remember craving is fantasising, it is imagining what it is like to take a dose of nicotine. An intricate but key part of this is that thinking of nicotine in the abstract won't make you crave. Non-nicotine addicts the world over think about nicotine, smoking, vaping etc regularly without craving nicotine. The key thing that separates thinking about nicotine from craving nicotine is entertaining the actual reality of consuming some nicotine. This is a key point so it is essential that you get it straight in your mind; the craving kicks in when we entertain the actual reality of having a dose of nicotine. I can sit here and think about nicotine to my heart's content without craving any because I know that I will not have some. But as soon as you start to think 'Actually, I could have just one dose' you will then think about the actual reality of having that dose, of the feeling of relief when the nicotine hits your blood stream, and you will then be craving. We will return to this concept later when we cover how to quit nicotine, but for now we will just consider it in relation to cutting down.

The problem is when you are cutting down you haven't stopped, so you know you will be having nicotine again. You may not be having any for ten minutes, half an hour, an hour, whatever, but you will be taking some again at some point. This means you are far more likely to crave nicotine if you are cutting down than if you quit entirely. There is a quote attributed to St Augustine that:

> "Total abstinence is easier than perfect moderation."

The usual outcome for those trying to cut down is that nicotine dominates their life even more because they are eternally obsessing about the next dose. The concept behind cutting down is to effortlessly and naturally want less and less doses. The reality is having to fight every inch of the way, to be constantly having to exercise willpower to postpone the next dose. You end up with more withdrawal, more craving, and more time thinking about nicotine and how much you want that next dose. This is the reality of trying to cut back on the intake of any drug. Of course it is only a matter of time before something happens, some incident or event, or one of those days that we all have from time to time when everything seems to just go wrong.

When this happens you're already getting to the end of your tether with the whole cutting down thing, you are sick of living a life of constantly wanting something but not being able to have it. When one of those days comes along, because you are suffering additional aggravation from the nicotine withdrawal (remember you only get rid of the withdrawal by quitting, not by cutting down) and because you desperately want to take whatever edge off the stress and misery you can, the entire attempt is abandoned. Usually ostensibly to be picked up again when things improve, but in reality we rarely return to it because we've just spent the time when we were cutting down convincing ourselves how awful life is without a constant supply of nicotine.

Cutting down is essentially experiencing those difficult first few days of quitting all the time. You don't get to have nicotine when you like, but neither do you rid yourself of the physical withdrawal. Most importantly when cutting down you are not doing that all important thing of learning to enjoy and cope with life without nicotine coursing through your veins

16. Should I Stop?

This may seem a bit of a pointless question. With all the health problems associated with being a nicotine addict the answer would seem to be self-evident. But most people are understandably more interested in the here and now than the future, so it helps I think to look at only the immediate short term benefits. Also when you start to understand nicotine addiction more fully, the pros and cons change dramatically.

Let's deal with the 'for' nicotine first. We've already dealt with the fact that the breathing in and the taste of smoke and vapour is not enjoyable, it only appears so because your brain links it to the relieving of the nicotine withdrawal. What it all comes down to when you strip away the ancillary parts is that the 'pleasure' is putting nicotine in your blood. So what is the actual pleasure there?

Ending the nicotine withdrawal is genuinely pleasurable. It turns you from feeling out of sorts, uncomfortable, unsure of yourself, groggy and woolly headed, to feeling alert, confident, resilient and sure of yourself. The problem is that you only get this benefit because you are relieving the withdrawal that was caused by nicotine in the first place. This aspect isn't actually a benefit of nicotine because it is the nicotine that caused you to feel out of sorts, uncomfortable, unsure of yourself, groggy and woolly headed in the first place. In fact it is the nicotine that will cause you to feel that way again. Indeed the only way to end that feeling permanently is to never take any nicotine again.

And that really is it in the pro-nicotine list. It will sharpen your mind and make you feel good, but not beyond how you would have felt had you never taken a dose to begin with. Indeed (and this brings us on to the cons of nicotine addiction) even when you're taking a dose of nicotine you don't feel as good as you would if you just quit, because nicotine is also eroding your sleep and your fitness. Both sleep and fitness have a direct impact on how you feel day to day. The best feeling in the world is not having a cigarette, or a vape, or a drink, or any drug. It is getting a full, decent nights sleep and doing a bit of exercise. Human beings are not meant to be sedentary, they are supposed to move. The more you move, the more positive and alive you feel. Nicotine robs you of that feeling, and it isn't just a feeling of being a bit more perky, you feel more confident, more resilient, and more able to cope with and deal with all the problems that life throws at us on a daily basis.

Remember also that the increased heart rate and blood pressure makes you feel lethargic, physically tired, and heavy. It is not a nice feeling, it is the polar opposite of that wonderful feeling of being healthy, strong and vibrant. And this is when you are actually consuming the nicotine (smoking the cigarette or inhaling the vape or putting the pouch or dip in your mouth) which is when you supposedly feel at your best. You get the worst of all worlds with nicotine; you quickly get used to the increased mental alertness so you need another dose to feel normal, but because it increases your heart rate and blood pressure, every dose will make you feel puffed out, heavy limbed and exhausted.

This is really the crux of it. Of course over time the effect on your blood pressure and heart rate will make you feel increasingly heavy and lacking in energy, will have a huge detrimental impact on your cardiovascular health, you will need more and more doses to obtain the same effect, and the cost (in terms of physical detriment and financial cost) will steadily increase.

You will have noticed that throughout this book I have referred to nicotine instead of smoking or vaping or pouches or dip etc. It is probably worth just mentioning smoking as compared to other methods of consuming nicotine. Vaping and pouches are often seen as a less destructive form of consuming nicotine than smoking as many of the toxins that are contained in cigarette smoke are not present. The problem is however that the method of consumption doesn't change the dynamic outlined above; any form of nicotine addiction gives all bad and no good. Or to put it another way, it gives a lot of bad, then removes some small percentage of it with each successive dose, and so creates the illusion of being an essential part of our lives. So even if nicotine had no adverse health effects at all it would still not be worthwhile doing. The fact is that it does have adverse health effects however you consume it. The nature of nicotine is that it speeds up your heart rate and increase your blood pressure and so makes you feel heavy and lazy and lacklustre. It erodes your fitness, it causes you to take exercise less (or at all), it causes you to overeat, it causes you to lose muscle, and it spoils your sleep. This is the nature of the drug, not the fact you smoke it by inhaling tobacco smoke which may have additional toxins in it. So whether you smoke, vape, dip, chew, snort, use gum or use patches, this basic dynamic remains. You get no good and a considerable amount of bad. Overarching all this, nicotine is a poison in and of itself. It is used as an insecticide; it kills living things. The doses we take it in are low enough that it kills you slowly rather than quickly, and I have no doubt that some methods of taking it are less damaging than others, but that's still no reason to take it. Vaping or using pouches and then justifying it by saying it's not as bad as smoking is like drinking arsenic and justifying it by saying that it's better than drinking arsenic with hemlock in it.

17. Why is it so Hard to Stop?

We've now covered off the basic dynamic of nicotine addiction. We've done this by breaking it down into its constituent parts and analysing each part independently and objectively. In this chapter we will put it all back together again and examine why it is so hard to quit, and the dynamics involved in abandoning an attempt to quit, using an imaginary person who has no understanding of how nicotine addiction works.

So Mrs X has decided she wants to stop nicotine. Let's assume for the sake of argument that she smokes cigarettes. She finishes her last cigarette, puts it out, and resolves never to smoke another. At this moment in time she is at her most determined, and you need to be determined when you are trying to do something difficult. But the problem is that as soon as the cigarette has been put out and she has exhaled her last breath of tobacco smoke, the nicotine starts to leave her body. Remember, nicotine has a half-life of two hours, so in two hours she has half the stimulating effect of the nicotine in her that she needs to feel normal, but it starts to drop the second she exhales that last breath of cigarette smoke.

This inevitable drop in nicotine results in two things. One we've covered previously and that is of course the withdrawal building up. So she starts to feel increasingly fuzzy headed, out of sorts, restless, nervous and generally more vulnerable. It is not a pleasant feeling and she knows it can be ended immediately by smoking another cigarette. She knows this both consciously and subconsciously and this is not affected by how determined she is to quit.

The second thing that this results in of course is that her confidence erodes. The nature of nicotine withdrawal is that it removes our natural confidence and decisiveness and replaces it with a feeling of timidity and uncertainty. This is a chemical process which causes an actual physiological mental response. This feeling of timidity and uncertainty will impact every aspect of your life, but of course the decision that is at the forefront of Mrs X's mind is her decision to stop smoking. So the physiological impact of the withdrawal has a double impact; it not only causes an unpleasant feeling that she wants to end, but it also removes any confidence that she had in her ability to quit. Of course over the next few hours the withdrawal steadily increases, as does the desire to end this withdrawal and the general feeling of uncertainty.

It is not just the physiological side of things that is kicking in now, but also the psychological. As soon as the withdrawal reaches a certain level Mrs X will get a subconscious trigger to reach for a cigarette. The subconscious triggers the desire for more nicotine when the withdrawal hits a certain level. This reaction isn't a huge problem, it is literally just a learned response to a certain feeling. It's exactly the same as tensing your right leg when in a passenger seat of a vehicle, you just ignore it and move on, but it can have quite a big impact on your decision to quit if, like Mrs X, you don't understand it. All Mrs X knows is that she decided to stop smoking and suddenly she wants a cigarette, and probably quite badly. She's already feeling nervous and is doubting her ability to quit, and suddenly she finds herself wanting to have one. Although this may seem like quite an obvious thing (to want a cigarette after you quit) it can be quite disconcerting because she now wants two completely different and contradictory things; she wants to quit smoking but she also wants to smoke. Because she doesn't understand where this has come from this confusion and uncertainty deepens her doubt.

The other aspect we now need to factor in is that at some point (it may be almost immediately after she has extinguished her last cigarette or it may be a few hours or even days later) the effect of FAB / ambition will kick in. Smoking is not now something she has, it is now very firmly in the 'I don't do that anymore' category. As such, she stops being critical of it and starts idolising it. If you concentrate you can pinpoint the exact moment it first comes into play. It usually manifests itself in the sudden realisation that there is a certain, special dose of nicotine that you will never have. You may suddenly think of Christmas, or a birthday, or an upcoming social event, or being on holiday and find you are panicking because you won't be able to sit out on your balcony of an early evening enjoying a cigarette, or a vape or pouch or dip, with a drink. You may be months from your next holiday, indeed your holidays may revolve around charging around after children rather than sitting around relaxing. But reality has nothing to do with this, because now we aren't looking at the reality of nicotine consumption, we're looking at it through the warped lens of FAB / ambition. We think of the past, we think back on it fondly, remembering only the (very few) good doses of nicotine. We don't sit there thinking about all the maintenance doses that we were scarcely aware of that made up the vast majority of our consumption of nicotine, we don't think of how our lungs felt tight and painful (if you smoke or vape), we don't think of the heavy lethargic feeling as our heart rate and blood pressure rocketed. We think of the future, we think of the idyllic nicotine situations where we won't be able to have nicotine any more, even though we may never have actually had nicotine in that situation anyway, and may never realistically do so.

We think instead about sitting outside a café in an exotic foreign city in the early morning sun, cigarette or vape in hand. How can we stop smoking or vaping and never have the joy of that? These are the thoughts that occupy our mind when in reality the chances are that this is something we'll never do anyway, and even if we did we'd have to take 100,000 maintenance doses over years before we even got there. And even if we did get there, what would the cigarette or vape add? It would make that experience wonderful by simply removing the withdrawal that was spoiling it in the first place. If it was the nicotine that was the special part of that scenario then why bother going to an exotic foreign city? Why not just sit at home and consume nicotine? Isn't it that the scenario is special and something to aspire to, but if we experienced it while in nicotine withdrawal it would be ruined, so the nicotine becomes a crucial element of it?

This is a good scenario to actually analyse to properly ascertain exactly what the nicotine would add to it, and what it would take from it. You'd be feeling groggy and slightly anxious due to the withdrawal and the nicotine would indeed make you feel confident and focussed, but this is something you would be experiencing all the time if you quit anyway, so it's not really adding anything. But more importantly what are you going to do for rest of the day? Not sit outside the café all day surely, you'll be bored stiff. You want to go out and explore, see the sights, walk the streets and narrow winding alleyways. Do you want to do this with a feeling of excitement, energy and enthusiasm? You won't be doing that if you have nicotine coursing through your veins. Think of that horribly heavy feeling nicotine induces, how it makes your limbs feel heavy and your heart race. Think of how it feels to sit down and consume nicotine and then stand up after, how it's then an effort to get up and start moving and you can even feel dizzy. The feeling that your limbs are made of lead and that you weigh about 100 lbs more than you actually do because your heart rate and blood pressure have gone up through the roof. No, that isn't old age, and no, not everyone feels it. It is a special feeling reserved for those lucky individuals with nicotine coursing through their veins. If, at any time in the future you look at someone taking nicotine and start to envy them, remember that feeling. Part of successfully quitting nicotine is to look at the reality and not let yourself drift into fantasy, but for now let's return to Mrs X.

Remember that Mrs X doesn't have any of this understanding, all she knows is that now she has the withdrawal, the triggers, the doubt, and is now thinking about how much she enjoyed smoking and how dull her life will be now she's stopped. Something is just missing. In fact why on earth did she want to stop in the first place? To avoid health issues that may or may not affect her in 20 years time? Who cares about 20 years time? Who can even think about having to go 20 years without a cigarette? And we haven't even covered all of it yet, because of course the other psychological process that is now kicking in is the craving. We've dealt with this several times in isolation and I have emphasised how powerful it is, but it really drives it home to consider its effect in the practical example we are going through in this chapter.

Mrs X is now thinking about smoking, in fact she's not just thinking about it, she's obsessing about it. She's starting to feel groggy and increasingly timid and anxious as the nicotine wears off. She knows that a cigarette will remove that feeling, so all she can think about is having a cigarette. She keeps thinking about how it would feel to actually smoke; that feeling of relief and clarity once the smoke hits her lungs. She's doubting her decision to stop, and she's thinking about how great her smoking life has been, and how wonderful it would be to smoke in future situations. And on top of all of this, she is now craving. This is perfectly understandable, after all she's decided to stop but now isn't sure if that was the right decision. So what does she do? She goes over the pros and cons of the decision again. How does she go through the pros and cons of smoking again? Well, she thinks about what would happen if she smoked. She thinks about taking the cigarette out of the packet, about the lovely firm feel of it, the smell of the dried tobacco, of putting it in her mouth, of lighting it and drawing a mouthful of smoke deep into her lungs, of the clarity and confidence it would bring. As soon as she reaches this stage, on top of everything else, the craving is in full swing. Now there is virtually nothing that can happen in her life that will draw her thoughts away from smoking, she is obsessing about it. She won't enjoy the parts of her life that she ought to enjoy, and I'm not just talking about holidays or the big things, I'm talking about sitting down at the end of a hard day, seeing friends, or going out for the day. She can't concentrate on work, on home, on her social interactions. Her whole life goes on hold while she travels around and around on a very unpleasant mental merry-go-round.

While all this is going on there is another element that also kicks in which ties back to our confidence / timidity. We dealt with this previously when we covered off that when we are feeling physically well this translates into a feeling of confidence, which makes us want to go out into the world and live. When we feel physically under par this translates into a feeling of timidity, we want to hide away and rest. When we are feeling confident we want to get out there and attack life. We want to face our problems and start batting them away. But when we are feeling timid and weak we want to hide from our problems, we want to hide under our duvet and leave our problems for another day because we just can't face them today. Because the withdrawal causes this feeling of timidity, which in turn makes us want to put off our problems and deal with them another day, a day when we feel more up to it, we very soon start thinking that we've picked the worst of all days to quit. This is why we go into the thought process of 'yes I do want to quit, but not now, now isn't a good time, I have the holiday / social event / difficult occasion etc coming up, it's far better I carry on with nicotine for now and quit at a more opportune moment'. This is in fact why the vast majority of attempts to quit fail. The withdrawal causes us to feel weak and unable to deal with anything difficult, so we have a natural tendency to put off anything difficult until another day, a day when we feel more confident and able to cope. The problem is that every time we quit we encounter the withdrawal so every attempt to quit has the odds stacked against it. We're not abandoning our attempt to quit, we're just putting it off until another day, a day when we are more likely to succeed.

The fact is that it is the withdrawal that creates this desire to put off dealing with our problems until another day, because we don't feel right. We don't feel confident and resilient and able to deal with our problems. We feel weak and out of sorts and this makes us want to put off anything difficult until another day. We have X, Y or Z at work, or at home, that makes now a particularly bad time to stop. 'If I can just wait until A, B or C is out the way it will be far easier.' We sense that we are not at our best so want to put off this difficult thing until we feel better. The trouble is that we never feel at our best when we quit, so from this perspective at least it is never the right time to quit. We've already dealt with how nicotine addicts need nicotine to cope with and to enjoy life, so while they have a life to live there will always be a reason to keep taking that next dose of nicotine and to put off stopping until another day.

Now we've looked at all these combinations of factors together and fully appreciate what an intolerable situation Mrs X is getting herself in to. We now have to add on to this that as Mrs X works her way through the craving process she will eventually get to the 'search for excuses'. There are two psychological elements going on here. Let's analyse these and then consider how they impact Mrs X's attempt to stop smoking.

Firstly when the subconscious decision to smoke has been made the physiological reaction will kick in. Mrs X will no longer just be feeling a bit woolly headed and out of sorts, she will have an intense almost panicked feeling to smoke, as her brain starts to recalibrate in anticipation of the incoming nicotine. The desire to smoke will be at its peak.

Secondly remember the 'search for excuses'. We have covered this off already but it is worth running through it again to help to place it into context in a practical example. The simple fact is that we can only think of a limited number of things at any one time. I have heard that humans can only think of 7 things at once. This means that you can actively think about 7 different things, then if then something else then pops into your head, you forget one of the original seven things. How accurate this is I don't know, I suspect it depends not only on the individual, but the nature of the things we are thinking about. Be that as it may, for our purposes I think it will suffice for us to accept that the human brain can only think about a finite number of things at any given moment.

Remember also that there is considerable evidence to suggest that what we think of as our decision making thought process isn't that at all. The majority of our decisions are made within a split second in a subconscious area of our brain, and in fact what we think of as our rational, conscious decision making process is simply us retrospectively justifying a decision that has already been made. Again you may or may not accept this theory, it is most certainly more likely to be true for some decisions than others, but again for our purposes I think we can agree that our decision making process is likely to exhibit unconscious bias, particularly in respect of decisions that accord us a considerable amount of short term pleasure (even if that pleasure is really just relieving something that is unpleasant).

Let's now apply all this to our imaginary Mrs X who is now feeling very uncertain, fuzzy headed, and timid. She desperately wants the comfort of the cigarette and is fully craving one. What is now in her mind is how much she used to enjoy smoking, how much her upcoming holiday / Christmas / birthday / social occasion is going to be spoilt by her not smoking. She is wondering how can she go through life never sitting outside a café in an exotic city smoking a cigarette (or whatever her idyllic smoking scene is). She is thinking about how she seems to have picked the worst possible time to stop, and that she could surely manage it if only she picks the right occasion. She is obsessing about how wonderful it would feel to draw that tobacco smoke into her lungs, how the cigarette will feel, and how crisp and fragrant it will be.

Most people who are reliant on nicotine will have attempted to stop and if this is you then you should be able to relate to this thought process. The details will be very specific to the individual (such as what constitutes your ideal nicotine experience, an upcoming event that you feel will be particularly difficult to navigate after you have quit, etc) but in general terms the thought processes are quite generic and are caused by the drives and reactions that all humans have. They are those driving forces that are designed to keep us alive and thriving but are confused and act to our detriment when we encounter drugs.

Above I have listed something in the region of 7 categories of thought that will be swirling around Mrs X's confused and doubtful mind. In reality there will be many more than 7 as each one will have its own specific subcategories and there may be additional thoughts (maybe her husband smokes and she wonders how no longer sitting down with him and enjoying a cigarette will affect their relationship, is she letting him down?) but they will all be concentrated on idolising smoking. Remember that we can only think of 7 (let's agree 7 for the sake of argument, although the actual figure may be slightly more or less), so every thought in her head is now on the side of 'start smoking again'. We base our decisions on considering relevant factors, but if we can only think of seven things at any one time, then we are actually basing our decisions on whatever 7 things are in our mind at any particular time. The decision therefore is a foregone conclusion; return to nicotine. After all, we're deciding on the basis of seven reasons to return and not a single one not to, because this is all we can hold in our mind at any one time.

The other point here of course is that Mrs X doesn't see smoking again as failing, after all she's not saying to herself that she will smoke again, all day every day, for rest of her life. Her mindset is just that she's picked a particularly bad time to stop, she can stop, of course she can, she just needs to pick the right time.

This thinking seems logical to Mrs X but when you understand the nature of smoking and nicotine addiction you realise how false it is. There is never a 'right' time to stop nicotine because as soon as you stop and the withdrawal kicks in all our confidence and resolutions drains away. We feel timid and weak and sense that we are going to struggle to do anything difficult. Therefore the natural tendency is to put it off until we feel better.

If Mrs X finally gives in and smokes a cigarette at this stage she will feel a whole world better off. She'll not only end the withdrawal (leaving her feeling more confident and resilient and able to face the world) but she'll also end the craving and the whirlwind of panicked thoughts that were flying around in her mind in a frenzy. Suddenly she is back to normal, feeling calm, confident, and ready to face whatever it is she has to do that day. A key point to note here is that of all that she was going through, the physical withdrawal was just a small part of it. Yes, it made her a bit groggy, took away some of her confidence and made her somewhat doubtful, but it was the explosion of thoughts and the physiological reaction that these triggered which was her real downfall. Any addiction is like a raging bonfire. With nicotine addiction the physical withdrawal is a modest match, the mind is the huge pile of dried wood and kindling that is the real source of the inferno.

So if it's this overwhelming how does anyone manage to quit? Well for most people the fact that they do want to quit remains firmly lodged in their mind, and most people (whilst not properly understanding the full mechanics) believe that time will solve the problem, that if they hold out long enough the desire to smoke will slowly ebb away. Some people are dogged or determined enough, or just sick enough of the whole cycle of misery that is life as a nicotine consumer, that they are resolved to quit no matter how awful and difficult it is.

Let's consider this in more detail by imagining that Mrs X is one of those people who manages to make it through the physical withdrawal. She will then be at the stage of no longer having any withdrawal. She will have the confidence and resilience all the time that the withdrawal was robbing her of. She will also be sleeping better, her appetite will have stabilised, she will find physical activity less repugnant, and overall she will feel far better than she ever did when she was smoking, even while smoking that first precious cigarette of the day. The problem is that this will all happen relatively slowly (usually from around 5 days to 3 weeks). The gains are substantial and positive, but slow. When you smoke a cigarette you feel better the second the smoke hits your lungs. It's so obvious you can't miss it. But when you quit you don't feel any different second to second, minute to minute, or even hour to hour. For this reason if you are not looking out for these benefits you can miss them entirely.

Another point to bear in mind is that you can crave nicotine without any physical withdrawal. If you want something, and can't have it, and you then sit there fantasising about how great it would be to have it, and how miserable you are without it, then you will be craving. So the craving can outlive the physical withdrawal.

In addition to this as time passes the effects of FAB kick in. The more nicotine recedes into the past the more fondly we think of it, and the more we remember the small amount of good and forget the vast majority of the bad. The more time that passes the more nicotine is put I the 'I don't have it' category which makes us idolise it and want it even more. As health, diet, fitness, and sleep improves, so does our confidence. We find it very hard to imagine the feeling of timidity and mental frailty that made it so difficult to quit. Just as it is impossible to remember very bad pain, to truly remember the actual depth and effect of it, so it is impossible, when we are feeling confident and capable, to remember what it is like to be weak and fearful.

So the passage of time may rid Mrs X the withdrawal, and she will be substantially better off, but she is unlikely to notice this. She is likely to still crave a cigarette on occasion, and all the while her memory of the misery of smoking will dim, and she will start to think more and more fondly of it. More importantly she will struggle to remember the timidity and frailty of mind that made stopping so difficult. At this point she may start to think that she has beaten it, that perhaps she can have one as a special treat, she won't get addicted again, how could she? She feels strong and confident and she's gone weeks without smoking, and even if she were to get addicted again she can just stop no problem. And so she could if only she retained her current level of confidence and resilience, but of course she will not remember the level of frailty and weakness and inability to deal with anything difficult that the withdrawal induced in her.

The subconscious triggers themselves can also continue for some time. Mrs X's subconscious has learnt from all her years as a smoker that cigarettes relieve stress. What it didn't factor into the equation was the key piece of information that the only stress that smoking relieved was the additional stress caused by the withdrawal; what it didn't do was relieve any of the stress caused by the stressful event in question. So any time Mrs X encounters any stress, her subconscious will jump up and tell her to reach for a cigarette.

For all these reasons time does solve some of the problems associated with stopping nicotine but only for other factors to kick in which increase her likelihood of going back to it. She will find herself thinking of it increasingly fondly and will not remember adequately what it was actually like to be fully in its grip.

Let's say Mrs X has now been some weeks, months or even years without a cigarette. One day she has, as we all do, a bad day. At this stage she has no withdrawal so a cigarette won't relieve any of her stress at all, but she doesn't know this. All she knows is that a cigarette always used to reduce her stress. She has also by now forgotten virtually all of the downsides of smoking, and remembers it very fondly. On top of all this she is feeling strong and confident; she can't quite imagine the frailty of character that made stopping so difficult. She starts to crave. If she lights up she will feel better, not because she is relieving any withdrawal, but because she's ended the unpleasant, purely psychological, craving.

Indeed under these circumstances she'll probably feel physically worse for having had the cigarette. Nicotine is a powerful stimulant and if you're not used to it, it leaves you feeling anxious and slightly nervous (similar to how you feel when you drink too much caffeine). It can even make you sweat and feel nauseous if you are not used to it. It will leave her feeling weak, heavy and lethargic. It will however have ended the distressing mental conundrum caused by the craving process, so overall she may well end up feeling better for smoking. In fact she could just have avoided or ended the craving process in other ways (which we will deal with later in the book) but she will not have known this. Remember that Mrs X doesn't fully understand the processes involved; all she knows is that she's had a hard day and a cigarette seems to have helped her. This experience will cement further in her mind that smoking is genuinely relaxing and helpful in difficult situations.

18. Withdrawal and Stimulation

So as things stand we have a fairly straightforward understanding of nicotine. It's a stimulant, your brain adjusts to it, so when it wears off you end up under par. The nicotine starts to leave your system the second you finish a dose of nicotine and so the withdrawal starts as soon as the dose ends. This is all well and good but how do we then reconcile this with other things we know about nicotine, for example that the first few hours of a smoker's sleep is disturbed by the stimulating effects of the nicotine. How can the stimulation effect still be there if it is already wearing off and causing withdrawal? This brings us on to a slightly more intricate part of the process.

When we take a drug we think of it having an effect on us; it wakes us up (in the case of caffeine and nicotine), or it relaxes us (in the case of alcohol). In fact drugs do not have single effects, they affect different parts of our brain in different ways, and these different effects run their course at different times.

Think of nicotine as having two separate effects; it gives us that buzz of making us feel more alert and focussed, but it also makes us feel anxious. It is a stimulant, and these effects are two sides of the same coin; the mental focus but also the increase in anxiety.

There are two ways we experience stimulants; a good way and a bad way. The good way is that we feel awake, focussed, positive, and alive. The bad way is that we feel jittery, anxious, and uneasy (think about when you might have drunk too much caffeine). Nicotine actually makes us feel both, but the bad from one dose is often scarcely noticeable. The trouble is that the good feeling wears off far quicker than the bad one. The good one wears off after a few minutes, whereas the bad one takes far longer.

Imagine that every dose of nicotine gives you one dose of 'good' stimulation and one dose of 'bad'. The 'good' wears off in 1 hour, the 'bad' wears off after 4 hours. After your first dose of nicotine you have 1 dose of 'good' and one dose of 'bad' inside you. The 'good' feels pretty good, and the 'bad' is almost imperceptible. After an hour though, the 'good' has worn off so you have another dose. You then have 1 dose of 'good' in you, but now 2 doses of 'bad' (because the 'bad' still hasn't worn off). The 'bad' may still be almost unnoticeable, but it has just doubled, so it is becoming more significant. As the day wears on and the doses of nicotine continually increase, so does that build-up of 'bad'. So as the day wears on you becomes increasingly uptight and irritable and stressed as the 'bad' builds up.

You may be able to notice this in your own nicotine consumption, but if not you will most certainly be able to see it in others, particularly if you study people who are very heavy consumers of nicotine. Look at these very heavy smokers or vapers or whatever. Do they seem relaxed, calm, confident, in total ease and in total control? Or are they generally stressed, manic and uptight? There was a reason J. Jonah Jameson was always shouting, stressed, panicking, and on the verge of a heart attack; it was the cigar permanently clamped between his teeth. I know that he is a fictional character, but like most fictional characters he is based on a stereotype born of our experience of real people.

I need to emphasise here that for most nicotine consumers, this 'bad' stimulation is there, but it is relatively minor. It will be impacting their lives; in how they feel, in the decisions they make (that constant feeling of insecurity will make them less likely to take braver, more courageous choices), but because it's there all the time they just accept it as normal. When we look at heavier consumers of nicotine though, the situation becomes more pronounced and more noticeable.

This can be a bit of a difficult concept to understand, so it might be helpful for me to describe it in a completely different way; how we experience life as a regular consumer of nicotine compared to how we feel after we quit. This is based on my own experiences and the experiences of many others who have been able to compare how smoking, vaping, etc made them feel while they were doing it compared to how they felt after they quit.

When you wake up as someone who is dependent on nicotine, you have a chemical imbalance in your brain. In essence your brain is used to having a dose of nicotine there, so it has a made a space, a void for it to fit into. When the dose of nicotine is there, you feel whole, well rounded, resilient, and generally speaking how you are meant to feel. But when it wears off there is a void, a space, an empty feeling that is crying out to be filled. Filling up that void is pleasurable. It is the feeling of being incomplete, of wanting something, and the feeling of then having it is the feeling of satisfaction, of filling that empty space. It's a false pleasure of course, because it is the 'pleasure' of removing something unpleasant that shouldn't have been there in the first place, but as we experience it, it does leave us feeling better off than we did before we took it.

After this initial hit is over, we feel normal for a spell, or at least we think we do. As a regular consumer of nicotine it is how we feel 90% of the time. But after you quit you realise that this isn't normal at all, because the residual stimulation is left over, and this leaves you feeling slightly anxious and jittery. In short it leaves you feeling less resilient and less able to cope, and more likely to be derailed or upset. Have you ever drunk too much caffeine? It's a horrible feeling; you feel agitated, apprehensive, and nervous. This feeling (albeit not as extreme as that) is essentially what is left over when you finish your dose of nicotine. It can be minor and almost imperceptible, but it is there.

The 'enjoyable' part of consuming nicotine may last about 5 minutes, you may not need your next dose for 20 minutes or half an hour or an hour or whatever, but almost as soon as you finish consuming that dose you will feel more anxious and uneasy than had you never consumed nicotine in the first place. This feeling of disquiet builds up the more nicotine you consume. This is why heavy consumers of nicotine are not relaxed and carefree (which they should be if nicotine actually relaxed them), but are more often tense and agitated. Start looking at other nicotine addicts and compare them to non-nicotine addicts. Start thinking about which of them looks more relaxed, more confident, more in control, more able to just shrug the minor irritations which make up our lives as human beings.

When you finally quit nicotine, you will find a feeling of confidence and peace that you haven't experienced since your first dose of it. Not only will this impact how you feel on a day-to-day basis, but it will also affect the course your life takes. It will unlock your full potential, allowing you to make decisions based on how you truly feel, instead of making decisions under a cloud of fear and insecurity.

When you are addicted to nicotine, you are not just going up and down through the usual cycle of drug addiction, rather you are addicted to something that, every time you take it, steals a bit of your peace and confidence.

There's another aspect to this which is worth mentioning at this point. We have already covered off that when we start taking nicotine we go through a period of being able to take it or leave it, but we can then never return to that stage. I am just going to take a moment here to recap this point, and then develop it further.

Nicotine withdrawal increases over time, reaches a peak, then tails off. It does indeed start as soon as you finish your last dose of nicotine but when it starts off it is almost imperceptible, but it increases steadily. It's not a particularly pleasant feeling but it can be a difficult thing to pinpoint, and it's simply an amalgamation of things we've all felt many times before; slightly tired, slightly dazed, and not being really with it.

When you first start consuming nicotine, the withdrawal will kick in, but you don't associate having another dose with relieving it. Why should you? If you've never taken nicotine during the withdrawal, you'd never know that another dose would get rid of that slight feeling of disquiet. Indeed you won't even think of that slightly out of sorts feeling as being nicotine withdrawal. This is exacerbated because the withdrawal takes both time and regular consumption of nicotine to increase in intensity. So when you start taking nicotine the withdrawal is slight and you simply wouldn't associate having another dose with getting rid of it.

But over time you will end up taking a dose during the withdrawal, and slowly you will learn that there is a certain unpleasant feeling that another dose of nicotine will relieve. You will learn this on both a conscious and a subconscious level, so over time every time you experience the withdrawal your brain will interpret this as 'I need a dose of nicotine; I need a cigarette or a vape or a pouch or some dip' or whatever.

The problem is that this knowledge is true; another dose will relieve the withdrawal. That is a simple fact and when you come to know this on both a subconscious and a conscious level you can never unknow it. You can quit nicotine for one year, ten years or fifty years, but no period of abstinence can make you forget what you now know as fact; that the unpleasant feeling that kicks in when one dose has finished can be relieved by taking another dose. You can never go back to how you were when you started because you can never unknow what you know now. You can never go back to that state of mind where you can experience nicotine withdrawal without knowing that another dose will relieve it, so you can never go back to being able to take it leave it. That phase is a once in a lifetime experience, it can never be repeated. Addiction is a one-way street, you can never backtrack.

Over the years we become increasingly attuned to the withdrawal. It needs to be less and less severe for us to notice it, and of course it becomes increasingly severe over time anyway. These two effects mean that there is a tendency to steadily increase our consumption of nicotine, as the withdrawal increases and we become increasingly sensitive to it. We get used to relieving the withdrawal at a much earlier stage. When we feed into this the craving process, the whole problem becomes amplified. We start to realise (either consciously or subconsciously) that when we start to think about our next dose of nicotine we stop being able to focus on anything else, so we just take the dose in order to keep focussed and engaged in what we are doing (be that talking to people, working, or just relaxing watching television). It's the same as having a chocolate bar or cake or something else you really want to eat but ought not to, sitting around at home. It's easier to just eat the wretched thing than having it sat their weighing on your mind, constantly singing its siren song.

For all these reasons the natural tendency with nicotine is to steadily take more and more, not less and less. As we take more and more the disadvantages become increasingly marked; the more we consume the more our heart rate and blood pressure increases, the more lethargic we feel, and the more anxious and disquieted we feel overall. Remember also that the only 'enjoyable' doses of nicotine are the ones where we have had to abstain for some considerable time (like the first dose of the day). The heavier your intake, the more doses are 'maintenance' as opposed to 'enjoyable'. The 'pleasure' decreases while the disadvantages increase.

19. Self-Image and Social Media

Self-image is a hugely important aspect of our lives. We think of ourselves in a certain way, and we act in accordance with that image. It dictates how we dress, how we act, and what we say. We not only act in line with our self-image, we also like to project it.

Have you ever seen an adolescent looking small and nervous, but with heavy metal garb on? They don't see themselves as we see them, they see themselves in the image of the growling beast on stage. A positive self-image is important. It makes us feel good about ourselves.

You may see people who you think look absurd, but they don't think they look absurd, they see themselves in whatever self-image they have, and they think positively about themselves. This is why shop mannequins and models on the catwalk are so important, creating an industry worth millions. If you see a model wearing a coat, and he or she looks amazing, you are more likely to want it, because you see yourself looking like that. If you are shopping for something and you see it on a shop dummy, looking sharp and neat and perfectly fitting the Adonis shape of the dummy, you think 'wow that looks good, if I get that I'll look like that'. You may look absurd in it, but in your mind you'll be seeing the shop dummy shape, or the model wearing it, and that is how you will see yourself.

Self-image isn't just about seeing ourselves in a certain way, it's also about projecting ourselves in that same way. These days, with everyone carrying a mobile device with a camera, with Facebook and Instagram, we are able to project our self-image like no other time in history. People spend great swathes of their lives taking pictures and uploading them for their friends to see: a picture of them out enjoying themselves, a picture of them smoking or vaping, a picture of them drinking, whatever. Why do people like to do this? Because they're projecting an image. They don't post pictures of themselves when they've just woken up in the morning, or on the toilet, or a picture of themselves riddled with despair as they contemplate the meaningless of their lives. They're not just trying to portray the image to you, they are also creating that image for themselves.

Smokers smoke. Vapers vape. Nicotine addicts consume nicotine. That is the nature of nicotine. Smokers believe that they have no choice but to smoke, vapers believe that they have no choice but to vape, so they try to make the best of it by creating a self-image that promotes a positive view of what they do. They do this in two ways. Firstly by showing themselves proudly smoking or vaping away, trying to make it look rebellious or masculine or feminine or whatever spin they want to put on it to make it a more attractive package.

Secondly they concentrate on images portrayed by others showing nicotine addiction in the same, positive light. This is why smokers and vapers like to see their own heroes and heroines smoking or vaping, indeed they often seek out such idols specifically because they smoke or vape. Of course these idols are themselves doing exactly the same thing; looking to project a certain positive image of their own nicotine consumption. This is why smokers and vapers like to post pictures of themselves smoking and vaping, and why they like to see images of others smoking or vaping; it helps them build in their minds the image of nicotine as mature, exciting, rebellious, different, adventurous, or whatever other positive little spin they may be able to tag onto their addiction which helps them to see it in a more positive light.

The problem is that this image is patently false. Nicotine makes people tired, lacklustre, often overweight, always unfit. The lack of exercise and poisoning of the body gives them a grey complexion. They are tired and weak. People may see nicotine as rebellious or masculine or feminine, but it isn't. It's the same as the 14 year old acne ridden 70 lb child with lanky long hair seeing themselves as the intimidating heavy metal icon.

I am not asking you to create an image of yourself as a smoker / vaper or a non-smoker / non-vaper or anything, but I am asking you to see through the nonsense and see the reality. Let's consider the reality of being a nicotine addict. Forget the mysterious, smoke laden publicity shots of the stars of the 1950s, of the images of young men and women looking sultry, moody, happy, successful, etc with cigarettes or vapes in hand. Forget the nonsense now and think of the reality.

Nicotine is a drug. It is dangerous and causes cancer and cardiovascular problems, but we keep taking it because although it's very bad for us and makes us unfit, tired, weak, lazy, overweight and out of shape, we have to keep taking it because when we stop we feel scared and unhappy.

That really is all there is to it. When you strip away all the nonsense that's what you have left. Yes I am aware that there are a very small number of people out there who take nicotine and are fit and strong, but these are usually people who haven't been taking nicotine for long, and who started off incredibly fit and strong, or have hard physical jobs that keep them in some kind of shape despite the effect of the drug. In short they are fit and strong despite, and not because of, their nicotine consumption. More importantly there is not one single one of them who wouldn't be far fitter and far stronger if they quit.

In fact virtually everyone these days knows that nicotine restricts people's lives and potential, and we know it at a fairly deep level. The problem is of course that despite this we still have to keep taking it, so we start looking at it from different angles to see if we can't see it in a more favourable light. Our smoking / vaping icons are a classic way of doing this; we see ourselves in their image, we see our smoking as rebellious, elegant, tough, cultured, dashing, cavalier, reckless, or amiable. This is ridiculous when you strip it down to what it actually is; getting a drug into our blood stream to take away the insecurity that it created in the first place.

One of the reasons we can get to this stage of self-deception is because withdrawal increases our stress, but nicotine decreases the withdrawal, and so reduces our overall stress, giving the illusion that nicotine relieves our stress, making life easier to cope with. Most people, as they get older, find their lives become more stressful. Many of us have children to worry about. Our parents age and we have to come to terms with their mortality, and with our own mortality, and then we get to the stage when we realise that in fact our best years are indeed behind us. We suddenly realise that our hardly articulated, but very deeply held belief that we are destined for great things is nonsense, that this life, whatever it is we are doing, is as good as it's ever likely to get. We are indeed one of the drones who live and die without our lives being marked in any way. These worries become the background noise of our lives, always there but rarely are we fully conscious of it. This causes constant stress but of course nicotine takes the edge off them (or creates the illusion that it does). In this way nicotine becomes no less than a way of coping with our own mortality and the futility of existence. We have some nicotine and suddenly things don't seem quite so bleak. That's why nicotine is so crucial. The beautiful truth however, is that that feeling of things not seeming quite so bleak, is a feeling you will have all the time when you quit. Of course you'll have bad days, everyone does, but these will be the exception rather than the rule. The life of a non-consumer of nicotine is good days, and some bad days. The life of a regular consumer of nicotine is all bad days, partially relieved only when you have a fresh dose of nicotine coursing through your veins.

Essentially, the phenomenon of posting smoking / vaping images on social media and our obsession with our smoking / vaping heroes and heroines both serve the same purpose; it is a way of justifying what we are doing, of normalising it, of portraying it in a far more positive light. Don't fall for it. See it for what it really is. Maintain perspective.

20. Nicotine, Alcohol and Other Drugs

A lot of people find that it is while drinking that they most want nicotine, indeed when we start nicotine we often only take it when we are drinking, and some people go a considerable amount of time only taking nicotine when they drink. There are some sound chemical and physiological reasons why alcohol and nicotine are so closely interlinked. There is also a lot of correlation between alcohol, nicotine and other drugs. This is what we will examine in this chapter.

In fact the relationship between nicotine and alcohol works two ways; those who consume nicotine regularly are more likely to drink, and drink more, and from the other side the consumption of alcohol can lead to nicotine becoming more attractive.

To start with the first of these (those who consume nicotine regularly being more likely to drink), as we've already covered the effect of nicotine is to leave us uptight and tense. Whereas nicotine is a chemical stimulant, alcohol is the opposite, it is a sedative. In other words it decreases or inhibits nerve activity whereas stimulants increase it. It is an anaesthetic and one of the things it will anesthetise is the uptight, anxious feeling we get from nicotine. In this way alcohol is more attractive to the regular consumer of nicotine than the non-consumer. The nicotine consumer suffers almost constantly from an anxious unpleasant feeling and alcohol will take the edge off this as it depresses these unpleasant feelings. Imagine drinking far too much coffee until you felt anxious and unable to string a coherent thought together, then injected some morphine to anesthetise this unpleasant feeling. The morphine would make you feel substantially better, far better than if you were to take it when you were feeling fine and had no pain or unpleasant feelings to relieve. This is in essence what the nicotine consumer does when they drink; they need something to counter the overstimulation caused by the nicotine and alcohol is a readily available and socially acceptable sedative.

There is another aspect to this worth mentioning at this point. Because nicotine raises both heart rate and blood pressure which in turn causes us to avoid physical activity, nicotine consumers tend to look for pastimes and activities that don't involve much physical movement, like sitting around drinking.

It is often the case that people who have concerns about alcohol and nicotine will look to stop alcohol first because this is often the more immediate problem in that it causes more instant and serious issues due to its intoxicating effects (so it can for example cause personal relationship and work issues in a way that nicotine may not). Some people find it more effective to quit nicotine first and then deal with alcohol because a substantial part of the need to keep drinking can be caused by nicotine. If you are concerned about your drinking (or even if you have no such concerns but are interested in learning about alcohol) then you may be interested in reading Alcohol Explained which provides a similar analysis of alcohol that this book provides about nicotine.

So much for the regular consumer of nicotine, but what about the other side of the situation, where people drink alcohol and find they want to consume nicotine?

Alcohol is a sedative, which means it leaves us dulled, uncoordinated and slow. Nicotine, being a stimulant, takes the edge off this and makes us feel more awake. So when people are drinking they will often want some nicotine to counter the sedating effects of the alcohol. It really is the most ridiculous situation, you take the alcohol to deaden your senses, then take nicotine to heighten them again. To what end? To feel exactly how you did before you took either drug in the first place.

The final point to mention in this chapter is that alcohol, being a depressant, is also an anaesthetic. Although there is a tendency to take more and more nicotine, there is often a physical restriction on our doing so. Smoking and vaping for example makes our lungs feel tight, our throat sore, and generally becomes increasingly unpleasant. The anesthetising effects of the alcohol take the edge off this meaning we can continue to smoke, vape or dip well in excess of what we might usually do. Let me be quite clear; it doesn't stop the damaging effect, it just means we can't feel it. So drinking allows us to relieve the withdrawal from the nicotine uninhibited by our body sending us messages of pain to indicate to us that what we are doing is killing us and hurting us

So the natural tendency is for our nicotine consumption to increase, and as it does, we suffer more from both the withdrawal and the overstimulation from nicotine, which leads us in turn to drink more to anaesthetise the effects of the nicotine, but it also leads many people to start taking harder drugs. The continued consumption of nicotine creates a feeling of never quite feeling right, of never quite feeling comfortable in your own skin. This creates a tendency to always be on the lookout for ways to change how you feel. Unfortunately, hard drugs are one of the options many nicotine consumers turn to.

21. How to Quit Nicotine

Nicotine addiction, in common with any chemical addiction, is essentially the result of our body and brain being tricked by the effects of a drug. It affects us not only physically, but mentally as well. The key to ending it is understanding. In the same way if I keep making the same mistake when trying to do something on a computer, full understanding gives the key to taking the correct actions to remedy the problem. Addiction essentially comes about because however much we know about all the bad sides of any particular drug, and however much we see all the harm it does us physically, mentally, and socially, we believe at a deep level that we need that drug to enjoy and cope with life. That is the very essence of addiction. It doesn't matter what terrible things a drug may do to us, if we genuinely believe that we need that drug to make our lives bearable and enjoyable we will keep taking it. When you understand that this reliance is an illusion you have taken the first (and most important) step in ending the addiction. I emphasise here that in doing this we can end the addiction, not spend the rest of our life resisting temptation or 'in recovery'. The key to successfully quitting anything is to no longer have any desire to take it. In this way we move from 'resisting' to 'genuinely not wanting'.

Fortunately a close analysis of any recreational drug shows that any benefits they confer are minimal, non-existent, and / or extremely short lived. It also reveals downsides that we are often not aware of. Further, much of what we percieve to be the benefits they convey are mere illusions brought about by our body and brains misinterpreting their effects. However illusion can be very powerful. Imagine if you lived a thousand years ago, that you are a fierce and strong warrior, and a wizened old man or old woman came along who could control the elements, the wind, the rain, the lightening, who could destroy your crops or make them grow, who could kill you with a single spell, who you could not kill and who would punish you and your family terribly if you even tried. You would live in awe and terror of such a person, their every word would be law. They would hold ultimate power over you. But imagine then that you learnt that every one of their spells, every one of their powers, were just a clever trick. That they held no magical powers at all. Suddenly they would go from holding absolute power over you, to you holding absolute power over them, after all they are actually weak and feeble and you are strong and powerful. This is the best analogy for any drug addiction. Knowledge truly is power.

We may feel that a certain drug has a hold over us, it can feel like it is an actual sentient evil being working to destroy us (hence phrases like 'the monkey on my back'). Some methods of stopping drugs involve seeing the drug as an evil being intent on killing you, and in quitting you are slowly starving it. In others you are encouraged to identify the part of you that wants to keep taking the drug, to call it your addict's voice, and detach yourself from it. It really can feel like these things have a life of their own. But they don't. Look at nicotine. It's just a drug that make us feel slightly different, more awake and focussed. It is in your absolute power to decide whether to consume that drug or not. Taking that chemical will have physical and psychological effects, as will stopping taking it. But the decision to take or not take is entirely down to you.

The purpose of this book is to provide you with a pragmatic and unemotional analysis of nicotine and the factors at play that keep you consuming it. When you have that in place your view of nicotine should be fundamentally changed. Have you ever heard about putting a copper nail in a tree? The idea is that the copper releases toxins that work their way slowly into the tree and eventually kill it. Knowledge and full understanding is the copper nail being driven into the tree of your addiction. But if you are intending to stop now there are a few other things to hasten the demise of your addiction and make stopping easier.

Firstly it helps to know exactly what you're in for. On the physical side remember that nicotine is a stimulant and your body and brain has become used to it. When you stop taking it, it will take three to five days for your brain to readjust and to get back on an even keel. However we are all different and this period is not set in stone, it may take slightly more or less. During this period you can expect to feel out of sorts, slightly dazed and groggy, you may well be more tired than usual, and you may find you want to eat more. You may feel restless, at a loose end, like that feeling you get when you can't relax because there is something you are supposed to be doing but you can't remember what it is. Try to allow yourself more time to sleep if you can, and don't worry too much if you eat a bit more over the next few days. Your appetite will soon return to normal and in any event when you stop taking nicotine you will very soon feel less lethargic and will naturally find yourself moving more. This more than compensates in the long term for any small amount of weight gain you may experience in the first few days of stopping. Some people (myself included) found it useful to not snack between meals. Eat what you like when you eat but snacking between meals can end up with you feeling uncomfortably full and frustrated.

When you stop you will also still be encountering the subconscious triggers. Don't forget that for however many years you've been consuming nicotine you have been teaching and reinforcing to your subconscious that when that groggy, out of sorts, anxious feeling of nicotine withdrawal starts to kick in, another dose of nicotine will relieve it. It can take some time for your subconscious to learn the new lesson; that nicotine is no longer on the menu. Just expect these triggers and don't let them phase you, remember that they are a very powerful survival mechanism that has been tricked into engaging because your body and brain is confused by the effects of the drug. Drugs are essentially poisons that feel beneficial even though they are not. Your conscious mind will know that you've stopped but your subconscious will take time to catch up.

These two aspects (the physical withdrawal and the subconscious triggers) aren't particularly enjoyable but neither are they of a magnitude to cause you a serious problem. You may feel slightly dazed and odd, and you will keep having the thought of nicotine popping into your head, but the real key is what usually follows these two processes: craving.

Remember that it is possible to think about nicotine without craving it. I've been thinking about nicotine in great detail for months since embarking on this book and I have not craved a dose once. The key tipping point between thinking about nicotine and craving it, is fantasising about actually having a dose and entertaining the possibility of having some. As soon as your thought process changes from thinking about nicotine in the abstract to thinking about how it would feel to have a dose and entertaining the possibility of having it, you will have moved into actually craving. Certainty that you will never have another dose can assist hugely. Certainty means that no matter what happens you never ever entertain the actual possibility of having another dose. So when you stop you need to make a solemn vow to never consume nicotine again in whatever form, come what may, and never ever doubt that decision. Craving isn't fatal to your attempt, but equally it isn't the best way to quit if you can avoid it. If you do end up craving there are two things you can do. The first is just wait. Cravings do not last for ever, eventually they will end and so you can just sit them out. The other way to get rid of a craving is to exit that frustrating, circular thought process. To do this you have to distract yourself. This can be hard to do but many people find that physical movement and taking themselves out of their current surroundings can help. Alternatively you can do anything that distracts you from this thought process; a hobby, a puzzle, work, a conversation with a friend, a game. We are all different and will find distraction in different things, so find what works for you. Always think of the reality as well.

Full understanding often means you won't crave because of course you only crave something you want. When you see through the illusion your view of the drug undergoes a fundamental change, essentially from something that you have to have in your life to something you are glad to be rid of. In this case you may be nervous about stopping, you may well be apprehensive and feel like you are taking a huge step into the unknown, but you will find that quitting is far easier than you anticipate and that your step into the unknown doesn't result in you plunging into the abyss. Rather it results in just another step forwards, albeit into a far brighter and more enjoyable future (with a few days of rapidly decreasing disorientation before you get there).

So ideally you won't crave, but of course we live in the real world, and you may end up in that frustrating and unproductive thought process. But there are ways you can guard against craving, and exit the thought process if you do start to go down that path.

Another effective way of ending the craving is to imagine the reality (and not the fantasy) of what would happen if you were to take another dose of nicotine. Remember all the factors at play; craving is about fantasising, it is a fantasy not the reality. When we've stopped nicotine the effects of FAB and ambition kick in, so we start to idolise it and forget the reality. So the first thing to do is to pause, take a breath, and think of the reality of taking that dose of nicotine. If you are in the first few days of stopping there will be some physical withdrawal to relieve. The physical withdrawal is not painful, it is just a feeling of being a bit groggy and finding it difficult to get on top of things. If you have nicotine you will gain only a partial short term reprieve from this feeling and in putting more nicotine in your system you will ensure that you will suffer that feeling again and again and again. Think of the feeling of the withdrawal as a cancer, a cancer you can feel inside you growing stronger and stronger while you grow weaker and weaker until it eventually kills you (in fact in terms of effect this is exactly what is going on). I have some medicine that can alleviate the symptoms, it can stop you feeling the full extent of this ever-increasing cancer, but it can only take the edge of it for a few seconds at a time. But the main problem with this medicine (apart from it being horrendously expensive) is that it doesn't actually stop the cancer, it only anaesthetises it while at the same time feeding it. So it may make you feel momentarily better, but it makes the cancer grow stronger and stronger and stronger, while you grow weaker and weaker and weaker (both physically and mentally). However the good news is that this medicine is the only thing that feeds the cancer; stop the medicine and the cancer will die, meaning you rid yourself of the constant unpleasant feeling of carrying it round with you, as well as saving your own life. Would you keep paying me huge sums of money so you can keep taking the medicine, to obtain some tiny, brief and partial relief, and at the same time make your cancer worse and worse until it eventually kills you? Or would you stop taking it? Most people would stop taking the 'medicine' even if it took years for the cancer to die. Fortunately you are far luckier than that because this particular cancer will be entirely dead in 3 to 5 days.

Remember what we dealt with previously, that from all the doses of the day you probably only really enjoy the first one; the rest are just maintenance doses. So if you do take that dose it may feel 'good' either by relieving an actual withdrawal that it created in the first place and will disappear anyway given time, or by ending the craving process that you could have ended through other means. But it will also feel bad because:

1. It will make you feel heavy and lethargic as your blood pressure and heart rate increases.

2. You will have a sense of failure and helplessness, because no matter how much you tell yourself you will find it easier to quit at some abstract future date, you know that that isn't true.
3. You will then be committed to taking all the other doses of nicotine that you are used to taking during the day, none of which will afford you the pleasure of the first dose, but will ALL have the adverse effects. None of the other doses will have the illusory pleasure that you are seeking from this first dose.

In short this partial relief would be the only 'benefit' of taking a dose of nicotine. But there will be other effects that are part and parcel of taking nicotine. You will also have the increased heart rate and blood pressure (with its long and short term effects), that feeling of heaviness and physical tiredness that comes about from having nicotine in your body. That is not a nice feeling and is a fundamental aspect of consuming nicotine. Think of how long the 'enjoyment' will it last for. A minute or two? Then what? It will be finished, you'll put it out, the nicotine will start to leave your system and in no time at all you'll be wanting another dose just as much as you did the first dose, but this next dose won't be in any way as enjoyable as the first. Consuming nicotine does not alleviate the desire for it, it creates it.

If you're craving nicotine after the first 5 days or so of stopping, then you won't even have the physical withdrawal to relieve so you won't even get that 'benefit'. As we've dealt with it's possible to crave something without any physical withdrawal. Because withdrawal from nicotine increases our overall stress, then partially relieves it, we are fooled into thinking that nicotine relieves stress. This means that for a period after stopping we will have the trigger to take nicotine every time we encounter any stress and this may well outlast the physical withdrawal. Again you need to think of the reality. Consuming nicotine when you are over the physical withdrawal won't even provide the relief from the withdrawal, in fact the stimulating effect of it will make you feel even more uptight and physically worse than had you not had it at all. But you'll still get the lethargy and the feeling of failure. And of course as soon as the nicotine from that dose starts to leave your body the physical withdrawal will return. Whatever stress you encountered will still be there, but now you will have the additional stress of the nicotine withdrawal, and so the whole nightmarish process will start all over again.

It can greatly help when stopping nicotine to closely observe other nicotine addicts. Remember that through your years as a consumer of nicotine you've felt that you've had to keep taking it, that life isn't quite the same without it, which is why you've continued to take it despite all the health problems, cost, and social pressure to give up. To justify this and to help you live with yourself you've built up a false image of nicotine consumption, that it's rebellious, different, masculine, feminine etc. Start observing nicotine addicts and test this image out. Are they generally slim, attractive, rebellious, masculine, or feminine? Look in particular at the older ones, as these are the ones who truly exhibit the effects of years of nicotine addiction. Don't they tend to be overweight, or painfully slim without being in any way muscular? I've noticed something I call the smokers stoop. When I was in the military I was taught to keep my back straight, my head up, my shoulders back and my chest out. It is how people stand naturally when they are fit and strong and confident. When people are feeling tired and heavy and weak, when they are feeling dejected and beaten and unable to cope, their head droops forward, their shoulders slump, their back curves forward, and their chest bows inwards. Nicotine addicts tend to have this stoop to them, it comes from the heaviness nicotine causes. Start looking at them objectively and free from the images you've built up in an attempt to put a positive façade on what is a very negative thing. Try to dispassionately see what nicotine really does to people.

I'm not saying that every nicotine addict stoops, or is overweight or lacking in muscle, but those who don't display these symptoms tend to be the younger ones who have not been addicted to nicotine for so long, so that these effects haven't yet become apparent. Look at people who have been taking nicotine for a few years, look at as many as you can and form your view from the majority of them rather than the minority. You don't need to take my word for it, but you do need to form your own objective view free from the prejudices you've built up so you can live with your inability to quit

The off-shoot of this is obviously self-image. Whilst we are taking nicotine regularly our self-image is that of a nicotine consumer and we try to present a positive image of this. Just as you need to take a dispassionate and objective view of other nicotine addicts, you need to start taking the same dispassionate and objective view of your own nicotine consumption. Forget your smoking / vaping icons / friends and the fantasy you've created around it, and see yourself (and them) as they actually are. Then start seeing yourself as a non-nicotine addict; someone who is fitter, more confident, more mentally resilient, someone who feels lighter and stands taller. Picture yourself and how you will react when those triggers to consume nicotine come along; when you are next out for a drink, or a meal, or at work, or at home alone, or whatever the situation is where you expect to receive a trigger to have some nicotine. Human beings have the benefit of imagination. We can imagine the situations where we would usually consume nicotine and we can sit and think and go through them in our mind before they happen. We can imagine how we will enjoy them and get through them without nicotine. In essence we can experience a situation before we even get to it. You don't need to turn up at the pub or bar and hope you'll manage without a cigarette or vape when the time comes; you can prepare yourself before you even get there.

This isn't something as ethereal as positive thinking, like when sports people imagine winning their event. I am never quite sure how effective this is anyway, if there are a dozen competitors all imaging themselves winning then the exercise must fail 11 times out of 12. This is a far more solid concept because it's not reliant on you having to be physically faster or stronger than other unknown people, it is reliant on one thing only; you. Practice makes perfect. If you go to a bar 20 times without nicotine you will be getting more and more used to it. You can work through these 20 occasions in your mind before you even get there for the first time. It may not be perfect, but its far better than just turning up unprepared and hoping for the best.

You and you alone decide whether you consume nicotine or you don't. No one can force you to take it. Every dose you've ever taken, you've taken because you wanted to. You may have had many reasons not to take it, and you may not have fully understood all the reasons behind both wanting it and not wanting it all at the same time, but nonetheless those reasons were there and were influencing your decision. However the decision is yours alone, it always has been and it always will be.

Make a solemn decision now to never ever take another dose of nicotine again. Often people seal this with one final dose; a cigarette or pouch or vape or whatever. This gives you certainty which will hugely assist your quitting. Know that every moment that passes you are growing stronger and better and happier and the addiction within you is slowly dying. Know that it is totally within your power to win this battle; your enemy is far weaker than you and is only able to trick you by guile; you can win by just never taking that next dose. Whether it is hard or easy, every moment that goes by your body and brain are repairing and becoming stronger. Knowledge is power, your enemy was able to keep defeating you because it knew tricks that you did not and could not understand, now that you understand its tricks nothing can prevent your escape.

If you have found this book useful and worth the purchase price, I would ask two things of you. Firstly and most importantly please tell other people about it. Ultimately all books live or die on the recommendations they do (or don't) receive. Secondly please take the time to leave a review on Amazon. Amazon is this books main marketing platform and every review makes a huge difference.

You may also be interested to learn more about another drug we regularly take without fully understanding it; alcohol. You may have no concerns at all about your drinking or you may be questioning your relationship with it. Either way it cannot hurt to fully understand it. Accurate and complete information gives you the best chance of making the right decision. Whether you're drinking daily, weekly, or occasionally, make sure that decision is the best one for you by arming yourself with all the knowledge and information you need.

Also by the same author:

ALCOHOL EXPLAINED

Alcohol Explained is the definitive, ground-breaking guide to alcohol and alcoholism. It explains how alcohol affects human beings on a chemical, physiological and psychological level, from those first drinks right up to chronic alcoholism. Alcoholism and problem drinking seems illogical to those on the outside, indeed it is equally perplexing for the alcoholic or problem drinker. This book provides a logical, easy to follow explanation of the phenomenon and detailed instructions on how to beat it. Despite being entirely scientific and factual in nature the book is presented in an accessible and easily understandable format.

ALCOHOL EXPLAINED 2 – TOOLS FOR A STRONGER RECOVERY

In Alcohol Explained 2 William Porter develops his insight into the alcohol phenomenon, and provides the tools you need to retake control of your life for good.

DIET AND FITNESS EXPLAINED

In Diet and Fitness Explained William Porter applies his logical approach to understand what hunger really is, why we favour some foods over others, and how we can retrain ourselves to enjoy a healthier and diet and adopt a more active lifestyle.

Printed in Great Britain
by Amazon

58549281R00104